RELIGION AND THE SOLID SOUTH

SAMUEL S. HILL, JR. WITH
EDGAR T. THOMPSON, ANNE FIROR SCOTT,
CHARLES HUDSON AND EDWIN S. GAUSTAD

RELIGION AND THE SOLID SOUTH

ABINGDON PRESS • NASHVILLE • NEW YORK

RELIGION AND THE SOLID SOUTH

Copyright © 1972 by Abingdon Press

ISBN 0-687-36003-X

Library of Congress Catalog Card Number: 72-175282

MANUFACTURED BY THE PARTHENON PRESS AT
NASHVILLE, TENNESSEE, UNITED STATES OF AMERICA

Dedicated to

EDGAR T. THOMPSON

Southerner *par excellence*, whose life and career epitomize both immersion in and transcendence of southern culture, and whose imagination occasioned the writing of these essays.

CONTENTS

PREFACE

The impetus for these essays was provided by a symposium, "The 'Bible Belt' in Continuity and Change," sponsored by the Center for Southern Studies in the Social Sciences and the Humanities, Duke University, in January, 1969. The principal figure in the symposium from its conception to the *postmortem* evaluations was the center's chairman, Professor Edgar T. Thompson. The task of cochairing fell to me at Professor Thompson's invitation.

The papers by Professors Thompson, Scott, Hudson, and Gaustad, as well as my essay "The South's Two Cultures," were first delivered, in earlier versions, at that time. In addition nine other papers were presented by the following professors: M. Gay Capouch, sociology, Case Western Reserve University; Christopher Crocker, sociology and anthropology, Duke University; Leonard Dinnerstein, history, Fairleigh Dickinson University; Thomas Hamilton, history, Old Dominion University; Berton H. Kaplan, public health, University of North Carolina, Chapel Hill; Weston LaBarre, anthropology, Duke University; Father Charles O'Neill, theology, Loyola University, New Orleans; James L. Peacock, anthropology, University of North Carolina,

Chapel Hill; Michael C. Thomas, sociology, Washington and Lee University (now University of Maryland); and Joseph R. Washington, Jr., religion, Albion College (now University of Virginia). In several cases, their material has been or will be published elsewhere in one form or another.

A second sponsoring agency, besides Duke University, was the General Council of the Presbyterian Church in the United States. The director of its research department (at that time), Dr. Samuel Southard, was an especially significant contributor to the success of the symposium. A number of other persons assisted as convenors, reactors, publicists, and hosts. As always with a conference, many people participated and facilitated.

After the symposium was over, the cochairmen felt both gratified and frustrated. The gratification resulted from the genuine achievements and the new directions taken in the study of religion in southern culture. But frustration loomed large because the topic, such a vital one for understanding the American South, has only begun to be tapped. A vast amount of work remains to be done. What is principally needed, however, is imagination—the isolation of the most productive devices for unlocking the mysteries of the South's culture, the formulation, perhaps, of new tools of analysis, the correlation of cultural elements heretofore thought of as unrelated, and the development of more sensitive eyes and ears on the part of researchers, whether they conduct interviews, prepare questionnaires, or read documents.

This book, accordingly, is a mere beginning. But it is that much, if for no other reason than that it is still one of a small number of books devoted to the religious dimensions of southern culture. In addition it is about the first book published which looks at religion primarily in its relation with other aspects of the culture and talks of religion in symbolic and functional terms. Perhaps these essays could not have been written had not the historians

10

and sociologists done the spade work. Now, as the work of the latter specialists continues, there must be much more undertaken by way of inquiring into the secular role of religion within southern society. Thus, students of institutions, belief-systems, symbols, values, social psychology, and no doubt other phenomena, must join hands to tackle a large task. I think Edgar Thompson is correct in his mature judgment that we have barely scratched the surface in perceiving the salient role played by religion for millions of southern people for more than two centuries.

I am deeply indebted to my fellow essayists. They met deadlines, reduced editorial work to near zero, and were always genial and cooperative. It is a pleasure to introduce them. Edgar T. Thompson recently retired as Professor of Sociology, Duke University, and continues living and working in Durham, North Carolina. Anne Firor Scott is associate professor of history at Duke. Charles Hudson is associate professor of anthropology at the University of Georgia. Edwin S. Gaustad is professor of history and departmental chairman, University of California, Riverside.

SAMUEL S. HILL, JR.
Professor, Department of Religion
Chapel Hill, N. C.
July 9, 1971

1
INTRODUCTION

Over the past 175 years the culture of the American South has occasioned more than its share of titles and nicknames, some of them humorous, others epithetic, and nearly all picturesque. Among those which refer explicitly to the religious dimension of southern culture, the best known is "Bible Belt." But this may be one of the least definitive, since the phrase applies to other American subcultures as well, and because the term which gives this book its title far surpasses it in descriptive power.

Of course "Solid South" usually points to the political homogeneity which persisted in the region from the 1870s until quite recently. As an indicator of the political situation, it continues to have some reality, though decreasingly so, with the effect that the term already has principal reference to the history of the South from Reconstruction until, symbolically, the 1954 Supreme Court ruling on the desegregation of public facilities. After all, southern voters have not comprised a solid political bloc in the last seven presidential elections. Moreover, the factions within the Democratic Party are so diverse that many, in quite different wings of the Party, are forced to reflect on the integrity of association with it. Do Klansmen, Wallacites, traditionalists like Stennis and Byrd, and socialists in fact belong to the same party? If so, many reason, perhaps partisan affiliation is a sham.

Geographically, no region which embraces both the Florida Gold Coast and Appalachia appears to deserve being called solid—and similarly, the Hampton Roads megalopolis and Black Belt Alabama, or northern Kentucky and downstate South Carolina. Are Atlanta and Knoxville really only two hundred miles apart? Is Atlanta actually in Georgia? Is the Virginia in which Arlington is located the same as Danville's or Suffolk's? Demographic descriptions of diversity are practically endless and, taken all together, seem to establish incontrovertibly the fact of an unsolid South.

On still another front, recent changes in styles of leadership suggest that the regional culture has become somewhat more liquid than our titular term implies. For many decades it was true that the range of faces seen among the influential elites was quite limited. Leaders began where their followers were by acknowledging the customs, values, and sensibilities of white southern society. By no means were they uniform, any more than the constituency at large was uniform. But certain features had to be present, if any popular resonance were to be expected. Whether in the political arena or church or education, to be effective one had to exhibit that he too was a Southerner. In public, at least, he did this typically with a sense of humor and anecdotal skill, both agrarian in tone, and a strong aura of moralism. It helped if he could inflect like an evangelistic preacher. One of the important developments in the past few years is the challenge to this homogeneity (or consensus) in leadership ranks which has been introduced by other groupings of Southerners who have lately acquired influence. Most prominent among these are blacks and educated young whites, but we must not overlook also smaller coteries of northern immigrants to Dixie cities and liberal middle-aged southern whites, among them some parents who have been taught by their college-student progeny. From 1607 to the 1960s the majority of both black and white people were inclined to subscribe passively to the infallibility of the accepted leadership. Moreover, since their minds operated with hierarchical images of order, they bowed to authorities. Now that situation is giving

14

way to another where less passivity is evident, and in which have recently appeared several new leadership groups and styles to contest the traditional consensus in taste and power.

These breaks with the southern past are paled by another and more basic fact of regional existence, however. This is the recognition that Solid South has historically referred to the white South—white people, their culture, their political and economic structures. Now that the black citizenry of the South has emerged as a first force in population and culture, the solidarity conception is in a shambles. Today, everyone knows that there are intense, even menacing, confrontations *within* the southern region. The traditional hierarchial arrangement has yielded to our time's awkwardly peaceful coexistence, and no one knows what the next decade augurs, whether reconciliation and mutuality or uncivil intramural strife. Moreover, the disappearance of the racially solid South—in the sense that norms, decisions, and leadership were determined by one race for both—is the only kind of break which is qualitatively new. All the other forms of diversity have their precedents in southern experience. To cite some examples: bourbons and populists have long lived side by side, as have rural people and urban people, agricultural and industrial systems, the latter day plantation economy and the yeoman farm–small business economy, even Republican and Democrat. Alteration in racial patterns stands alone as novel and truly innovative.

In the 1970s and thereafter, Solid South will be used less and less except to point to the past, because it will be more and more inaccurate, I predict. For reporting empirical behavior, the term has not been a particularly apt metaphor for some decades now, as we have seen. Nevertheless in other very important respects, Dixie was discernibly of a single piece for more than a century, and as far as popular culture is concerned, partially retains that character. These other respects are cultural, a claim which requires careful explication, by way of historical illustration throughout this volume and as definition and theory of culture here and in succeeding chapters, especially the second, which is entitled, "The South's Two Cultures."

In the antebellum period, Yankee and (white) Southerner alike could generalize about the land below the Mason and Dixon Line as the special preserve of a proslavery, agrarian, and aristocratic society. Residents of the South were given to describing themselves by contrast with other Americans, and to insisting on the righteousness of their distinctive heritage. Much of their identity was established by dissociation. Then from 1861 to 1865 the region was legally a separate nation. Following the war, the South stood aloof to the national mainstream, being concerned to heal its wounds, restore its dignity, and discover new ways of institutionalizing its traditions, thus conceiving of itself as a subculture apart. In the 1920s, further retrenchment took place as "a strange new world of urban booms and farm distress" served to clamp the lid on freedoms of feeling and speech and on tolerance in favor of a surprising latitude of conformity. Since the focus of this volume is on the religious dimension of southern culture, George B. Tindall's interpretation of the situation in that decade is unusually significant: "To a greater degree than the Ku Klux Klan, the fundamentalist crusade contributed to a revival of sectionalism in the 1920s. It stirred the Middle West to some extent, but unlike the Klan it scored victories only in the South—and the Scopes trial took place in the South." [1]

Although developments have been rapid since the presidential election of 1968, not to mention the fact that we cannot predict the mood and behavior of the country during the next presidential election year, the persistence of the George Wallace phenomenon and of Richard Nixon's "southern strategy" suggest that southern culture as a wide-

Introduction

spread, publicly visible variety of American life is far from dead. It seems to me that no other region of the United States could produce and present a public figure whose whole ideology and style are so recognizably regional. Nor is this contention gainsaid by the considerable electoral strength of the Alabama governor outside his territory. The salient point is that in the South, especially the Deep South, many Wallace votes were cast by public-minded, substantial, college degree-holding citizens who regarded his program as progressive and obviously in the best tradition of the republic. (It is instructive to compare Wallace with another "conservative," Barry Goldwater, to note that the Arizona senator was the legitimate nominee of a major political party and that his supporters included people with classical, thoughtful, widely respected, positive-minded positions.)

All of this is by way of contending that there still is a South, a self-conscious and publicly identifiable culture.* That is what "solid" connotes in the context of this vol-

* The persistence of the South as a distinctive culture is demonstrated in a recent study done by a University of North Carolina sociologist, John S. Reed. Presented as a doctoral dissertation to Columbia University in 1970 (and scheduled for publication in 1972), it bears the suggestive title, "The Enduring South: Subcultural Persistence in Mass Society." Professor Reed's inquiry, based on Gallup Poll national sample surveys conducted between 1938 and the mid-1960s, has to do with cultural qualities among white people of a similar sort to those treated in this volume, rather than with political and economic patterns. He focuses upon three of these: southern localism, southern violence, and southern religiosity. His conclusions, briefly summarized, are: cultural differences do exist between Southerners and other Americans; most of these differences are substantial; they are not correlated simply with the fact of the South as an agrarian folk-culture; and these differences have not decreased appreciably in the recent past. Incidentally, a number of specific contentions made in this book are corroborated by Reed's data.

17

ume. Although less dominated by a single pattern than formerly, and more susceptible to pluralization than from 1830 to 1950, the South persists as a coherent collection of assumptions, values, traditions, and commitments. If we define culture as Clifford Geertz does—"an historically transmitted pattern of meanings embodied in symbols, a system of inherited conceptions expressed in symbolic forms by means of which men communicate, perpetuate, and develop their knowledge about and attitudes toward life"—southern culture is still in evidence.[2] It embraces the perspectives and loyalties of several million (white) people concentrated from Little Rock and Shreveport to Jacksonville and Richmond.

To conclude that the South is rightly characterized as solid by these analytic means brands this study as distinctive from most. For such approaches either escape the notice of or are inconsistent with the methodological canons of empiricists who look for discrete data, that is, of most historians, political scientists, and survey research-minded sociologists. Such analysts would have grounds by their own standards for judging the South to be solid only if concrete evidence, like consistency of voting records or uniformity of racial attitudes, were available. But the significance being accorded "solid" here has to do with the more complex and multidimensional analysis common to anthropologists, social psychologists, and macro-sociologists, especially those indebted to Emile Durkheim whose work dealt with the comprehensively social, or wholistic. "Solid South," as I am using the metaphor, is essentially a qualitative reality, whereas those who speak of its disappearance usually base their conclusions upon quantitative evidence.

Turning to a very different issue, conventional religiosity, let us note the remarkable homogeneity of ecclesiastical and theological patterns in the South, and a companion datum, the contrast between the situation of the South and that existing anywhere else in the United States. The peculiarity of demographic patterns has been demonstrated by geographer Wilbur Zelinsky; the South is one of the seven "religious regions" in the country, with a typical Baptist-Methodist strength (sometimes in reverse order) from the Potomac to the Rio Grande, with astonishingly few exceptions.[3] In this volume Edwin S. Gaustad highlights the religious demography of the South and places it in historical context. From the angle of institutional statistics and dominance, religious patterns do have an impressive commonality across the southern territory.

But it would be theoretically possible for any given denomination to vary so significantly from place to place in its effects and influence that institutional strength and ubiquity prove to be quite misleading facts. For example, it is entirely conceivable, at the level of effects and influence, that Methodists in Texas have more in common with Presbyterians in Virginia than with their fellows in Georgia. The question therefore must be raised, is there relative congruency of images, loyalties, and priorities within the single denominations which predominate. Only if the answer is in the affirmative can we suppose that there is any degree of solidarity in what the churches formally teach as the shape of reality and the correct way of life, that is, in its proclaimed theology and ethics. Determination of solidarity in belief-system is a difficult matter, but one suggestive means is available in a study by Herbert W. Richardson, entitled *Toward an American Theology*.

A cogent conclusion drawn by Richardson is that there is an American theological tradition, which stands in marked contrast to the pervasive strands in European Christian thought.[4] Simply stated, in America emphasis has fallen upon the cultivation of personal holiness, building the kingdom of God on earth, the activity of the Holy Spirit in people's lives, and the principle of incarnation, Christ's real presence in this world. The central question here has been *cur creatio?*—for what purpose did God create the world? as distinct from the European preoccupation with *cur deus homo?*—why did God become man? which reflects an overriding concern with such themes as sin, crucifixion, and redemption. As a general interpretation, Richardson's contention carries credibility. Exception may be taken to it because of its exclusive attention to formal theology, which is never synonymous with the operative symbol-systems of people in a religious culture or religious institutions. However in the American instance, theology has been formulated not by an elitist class of university-based intellectuals, but mostly by pastors working out of practical experience—from the Puritans to Edwards to Finney to Bushnell to Rauschenbusch to Reinhold Niebuhr. Theology in this country has been usually closely linked with the masses of the people.

If we accept Richardson's thesis concerning American theology—that it exists and what it is like, we do so at the apparent peril of the thesis just developed, that the Solid South is made so, at least partly, by a coherent theological tradition confined within the South's borders. The problem arises from the fact that "southern theology" departs from this American theology in that it does not feature worship and incarnation in preference to sin and crucifixion. On the contrary, southern preaching and teaching are centered in the themes of man's depravity, Christ's atoning death, and the assurance of salvation. At the same time, however, members of churches in the South hear a great deal about the intimate presence of the Holy Spirit, sanctification, and building the kingdom on earth. Intriguingly, then, southern theology, while unique, thus divergent from both American and European patterns, has much in common with each. To a greater extent than mainline developments in this country, Christianity in the South founds meaning and responsibility upon the depravity of man and the atoning, effectual death of Christ on the cross, an orientation it shares with classical European thought. On the other side, the South's variance from European perceptions and modes is dramatic. After all, salvation understood as a state entered through a conversion experience, and the virtual equation of Christian holiness with abstinence from personal vices is a far cry from the Protestant interpretations of gift and responsibility prominent in Europe. Moreover, the notion that constructing the kingdom is a natural result of the conversion of individuals aggregated in society sharply demarcates southern views from European where concepts like Christendom and Christian civilization prevail. Associated with this difference is the contrast between southern theology's convictions about the "spirituality of the church," that is, its deliberate disengagement from secular matters in the interest of "minding its own business," and the historic commitment of much European theology to participation in and judgment upon the structures of society.

The oblique usefulness of Richardson's thesis for an understanding of the reigning theology of the southern churches consists in its highlighting the South's departure from the American mainline. Southern theology simply does not accord with what he describes, insightfully, I think, as American. Yet it is important to note that the same optimism about and devotion to the transformation of this world is characteristic of both traditions in the United States. The modes of the representative American theologies certainly differ from those of the popular southern churches (and from American mass evangelists whose cultural affinities are with the South), but the goals and expectations are similar. One can no more imagine southern evangelicals than Connecticut's Bushnell or New York's Rauschenbusch expecting that only the Eschaton will achieve history's goals. Christians are told that there is ever so much that can and must be done now, even if we all have to await the final consummation that southern preachers have so much to say about.

As a final word in this introduction, it should be pointed out that this volume is the product of five professional academicians who go about their labors in highly diverse fashion. Beginning, in the southern manner, with the lady, Anne F. Scott is an American social historian with a primary focus on women in American society. Charles Hudson is a cultural anthropologist whose present labors are concentrated on American Indians. Professor Edwin S. Gaustad's field is American history; he teaches at the University of California, Riverside; his specialty is the religious dimensions of our history. Edgar T. Thompson's primary sociological research has been in racial patterns and structures. I am a student of religion, particularly religion in American culture.

From our several perspectives, we join in underscoring (1) the distinctiveness of religious life in the South, (2) the domination of Christianity there by one of its families, Evangelical Protestantism, and (3) the role of religion as conservator and reinforcer of, as distinct from agent for change within, popular (white) southern culture. Consequently the ascription of solidarity, in this chapter's sense of cultural solidarity, is the only honest opinion available. As we shall see, it is one of the minor ironies of ecclesiastical and American social history that a religious tradition so desirous of being change-oriented should serve as a powerful force in keeping tradition intact for so many decades. The subject of these chapters, consequently, affords us a fresh and potentially rich investigation of religious phenomena and of the American South.

NOTES

1. George B. Tindall, *The Emergence of the New South, 1913-1945* (Baton Rouge: Louisiana State University Press, 1967), p. 208.

Introduction

2. Clifford Geertz, "Religion as a Cultural System," in *The Religious Situation, 1968,* ed. Donald R. Cutler (Boston: Beacon Press, 1968), p. 641.

3. Wilbur Zelinsky, "An Approach to the Religious Geography of the United States: Patterns of Church Membership in 1952," *Annals of the Association of American Geographers,* LI (June, 1961), 139-93.

4. Herbert W. Richardson, *Toward an American Theology* (New York: Harper, 1970), chap. 5.

2
THE SOUTH'S TWO CULTURES

In the Introduction alteration in racial attitudes and arrangements was set forward as the fundamental distinctive of recent southern experience. There we noted that changes in the relations between black and white people constitute the only unprecedented development in the current era of rapid social change. Beginning from that assumption, the present essay will contend that particular racial traditions and practices have served as the cement for the South's cultural cohesion. Other features have helped to provide a sense of separateness and to distinguish it among American regions, but they are consolidated by the racial factor. Wherever the South exists as a specifiable culture, the pattern of white supremacy, whether aggressive or residual, stands as its primary component.

This book's orientation toward the role of religion in southern culture requires that some correlation be established between the religious life of the people and these decisive racial features; otherwise the religious dimension might be construed as peripheral when such is not the case. How are race and religion correlated in southern experience? Two facts concerning the religion of Southerners stand out. In the first place, they take their religion seriously. They entertain scant doubt of the ultimate truthfulness of the Christian claim, a trait reflected in the high proportion of the population having formal affiliation with a church and by the absence of ideological alternatives. (Gaustad's chapter demonstrates this dramatically.) Few societies in modern Christendom can compare with the American South for proportion of religious affiliation or intensity of religious conviction. The second unavoidable fact is the rootage of Christianity, the religion the people embrace so zealously, in the claim that love is the ultimate power and purpose of reality, and the norm for human behavior. No serious reading of Christian teaching can challenge the conclusion that in its preachments concerning both the divine government of the world and man's call to responsible living, the central, all-dominating motif is love defined as creative good will.

If then the people of the American South can be said to owe supreme loyalty to a religious faith which accentuates love of God and neighbor, how does it happen that racial discrimination can have been practiced for so long by so many? Putting the question more fruitfully, what brought about the peculiar relations which prevail between the *two* cultures, Southernness and religion, in which the love ethic of the latter is modified by the values of the former and largely accommodated to them? It is important, if also difficult, to describe this strange interrelation—this paradox—and to offer some explanation for it. But we must begin by disregarding any argument which maintains that white Southerners have been typically insensitive to the needs and feelings of people. Nor does it advance our understanding of the paradox to impugn them as egregiously immoral people, either inherently or by comparison with other societies. On the contrary, their reputation for hospitality and friendliness is often supported by the quality of life they embody. They do prize helpfulness, courtesy, and amicable relations. Of course the temptation to romanticize southern society must be resisted, inasmuch as mores of this kind are common to simple societies. Even so, one is impressed by the lengths to which sons of Dixie are frequently willing to go for the sake of cultivating warm personal relations, in the process manifesting admirable grace and charm.

Morally, they have often acted with courage and resolution in expressing concern for public problems, for example, the adverse effects of alcoholic beverage consumption, gambling, crime, encroachment on Sunday rest, and so on. As Anne F. Scott's chapter demonstrates, numbers of humane causes have been generated by Southerners in such areas as educational opportunity, prison reform, and the establishment of eleemosynary institutions. They are a people whose hearts can be touched, who can be appealed to for the alleviation of human distress, whether they perceive this rightly to take the form of Christianizing the heathen in foreign lands or relieving misery at home.

Yet these same God-fearing Christians have subscribed to white supremacy. It is true that many of the most conspicuous advocates of racism are classifiable as "red necks," people who are not governed by good will and a noble sense of responsibility for others. But this is by no means the whole picture. Without flamboyance, the educated, the magnanimous, the religious also practice white supremacy. One does not need to harbor feelings of hate or be driven by destructive impulses to practice discrimination, after all, and millions of such persons have lived in the South. Whence and why the shocking contradiction that generous, benevolent, and amiable Christians are racists?

This paradox of southern churchmanship must be examined on both of its sides if we are to probe its depths and true character. The racist side is well known to sensitive observers. But it is no less necessary to see to what lengths and along what specific lines the southern churches have lived with a sense of social responsibility. In speaking of them we are not dealing with people who have been uniformly either cruel in their execution or vacuous in their perception of how life ought to be lived. The region's religious leaders, according to their own convictions and in their own ways, have frequently involved themselves in issues which have been directly related to the internal life of the churches. That is, the creed of many has transcended the common notion of the "spirituality of the church"— that the church should confine itself to preaching and teaching the Gospel and cultivating religious growth in its members, steering clear of secular involvements and objectives. The most prominent investment of church crusading has been toward the control of liquor sales and use. Look upon this issue as one may, it is partially social in character, a component in public morality, and southern churches have endeavored to render a social service by directing its supervision. For readers familiar with the history of Christianity, it is instructive to draw a contrast with the classical Anabaptist communions which have kept their absolute convictions on various moral matters within their own ranks, abstaining from efforts to legislate morality by imposing their views on the wider society. The churches of the American South have not been asocial or apolitical, rather, selective in the public causes to which they have devoted their passions.

The importance—and subtlety—of the prevalence of a sense of social responsibility within the churches of the South is well illustrated in a collision which took place in Lubbock, Texas, in 1932, pitting the conservative Protestant clergy against the issue of academic freedom on the campus of Texas Technological College.[1] What generated the clash was the activity of a few faculty members and YMCA staff, several having been trained in the tradition of theological liberalism at the University of Chicago, who were acquainting students with the ways of heterodoxy, socialist economic and political views, and modern academic skepticism. When two consecutive ministers of the huge First Baptist Church, the fundamentalist superintendent of city schools, and other religious leaders learned of the religious and social heresies being promoted under their

27

noses, they mounted an assault upon the Tech staff members, eventually securing their dismissal. (They were able to do this in spite of the tenured status of one of them, who happened also to be a departmental chairman.)

These events of the early years of the national depression on their face do not suggest that the ministers in question were assuming any social obligation. In fact we might initially conclude the opposite. But, on a closer look, it appears that they, perhaps especially the two ministers of a two thousand member congregation numbering many of the community's most influential citizens, endeavored to act in what they judged the highest interests of their society. For these and many other religious conservatives, the essence of social responsibility is the preservation of orthodoxy, primarily religious, but with social orthodoxy in a supporting role, as we see in their own words: "All our troubles, hard times on the farm, our present drought, all —are caused by sin"; "Christian people of this nation are going to have to take a definite stand (against evolution) some of these days and the sooner it comes the better"; the liberals at the college are seeking to "subvert the moral code."

Without being able to rationalize their instincts, in all probability such leaders saw clearly the need for a culture-ethic, that is, a framework of meaning and order for fruitful life in the society. They looked with disfavor upon pluralism. Moreover they were convinced that a people's greatness stems from purity in private morality among individuals and from God's systematic blessing of those who adhere to doctrinal orthodoxy. Rightly then they crusaded to eradicate "poisonous propaganda" and loose morality, *for the good of the civilization,* not alone of the churches. Southern religious leadership in Lubbock, Texas, in 1932, and generally throughout the South during this century especially, has perceived more than it knew in working to establish orthodox religion as the basis for a culture-ethic.

28

An item in the bulletin of a Lubbock church on November 8, 1929, speaks volumes: "Evidently God has a special mission for the First Baptist Church. She stands in a strategic place in a strategic section of the nation. This section is being filled by emigration from the great Anglo-Saxon centers of the South. . . . We have a pure-blooded, homogeneous population that can be directed into a remarkable social order."

This Lubbock scenario provides us with a set of conditions exceptionally transparent to the intimate correlation between the South's two cultures, regionality as (simple) culture and religiosity as cultural system. What the Lubbock fundamentalists set out to do, in the terms of this analysis, was to legitimate, consolidate, and perpetuate the secular culture through the instrumentality of conservative Protestant Christianity. Intoxicated by the growth of west Texas, yearning for stability and approval, needing a feeling of cosmic significance, and in quest of both comfort and scapegoat during a stressful economic period, religious spokesmen ballyhooed the status quo—practices of speech, dress, eating, organizing, doing business, racial relations, ideological preference, education, and the like. All threats to conformity and to recognition of their mores' superiority were to be resisted. The most effective device for sealing and confirming, one eminently accessible and universally approved, was orthodox Christianity—of the fundamentalist sort. It was the cultural system needed to tighten and sanctify the culture. That is, religion provided a formulated, coherent framework of meaning for ordering the west Texas culture which, like all cultures, was largely an accident of historical circumstances, migration patterns, geography, climate, politics, social conditions, and so on. Fundamentalist Protestantism when imposed upon the culture thus had much to recommend it functionally. It performed two complementary roles by providing a culture-ethic for ordering life in the society, and casting legitimation in the mold

29

of ultimate truth. Mentalities and sensibilities in Lubbock, and elsewhere analogously, have been locked in by the powerful double grip of secular effectuality and metaphysical confirmation.

In the context of southern society, often it has been especially difficult to discover viable arrangements for the maintenance of constructive social patterns. Life has had to go on, of course, but sometimes under taxing conditions, produced variously by racial strains, the challenge of developing stability in a frontier setting, and severe economic hardship. Historian Avery Craven marshals considerable evidence pointing to the "frontier" nature of antebellum southern society, from the Atlantic to the Mississippi.[2] Thus Lubbock's case may not be so exceptional, despite its rather late date and its situation on the territorial "edge." We may then take rather seriously Merton Dillon's interpretation of the churches' functionality in that burgeoning frontier city.

. . . the church served from the beginning as a means of social control. As one of the few institutions which impinged upon a large portion of the community, it lent itself well to such use. Life in a new country has always given some men an opportunity to shed conventions and restrictions; as they step from the threshold of ordered society, they are tempted to leave its trammels behind. . . .

There is ample evidence to suggest that the leaders of Lubbock from the beginning looked upon churches not alone as a means for assisting souls otherwise lost to enter the kingdom of God or as a means for gathering together the saved remnant of humanity, but also for the secular purpose of molding the social order. The churches were not to be set apart from the world; they were to be placed directly in the midst of it. Ranchers and a few merchants, most of whom were also church leaders, dominated the town. They and the preachers joined in the enterprise of creating an orderly community safe for churches and secure for business enterprise.[3]

Having seen something of the churches' involvement in responsibility for the culture's well-being, we return directly to the paradox, the practice of racial discrimination by a people who affirm love as the norm for human behavior. It is incumbent to recall that a variety of factors in southern life have helped stifle the influence of Christian teaching with respect to the immorality of slavery and segregation. First, the aftermath of the Civil War was a critical period in that the perceptions and aspirations of white people obligated them to defend their accustomed ways by hardening the lines of separation between the two races. The formation of Jim Crow laws was necessary for white southern society to achieve self-respect, a major point demanding fuller elaboration presently. A related though somewhat different matter is the observation of most whites, according to their own criteria, that the Negro is inferior. In empirical terms, especially by white standards, it is simply the case that the achievements of black people are sparse. To this day there are multitudes of whites who have never seen an accomplished member of the Negro race—except by means of television, a fact which itself is beginning to make a difference. In the southern social context, to see is to believe; perhaps examination of the causes of the black man's empirical inferiority would be far too painful to engage in, so that avoidance of subtleties has been a means of self-defense. Also, living as he has in a relatively homogeneous culture, the white Southerner has had little incentive to acknowledge the inherent strengths of a culture (the southern black) different from his own. It has been typical of folk-cultures to build figurative walls around their own, and to be uncomfortable over awareness of alternatives. Finally, the economic and political emergence of the blacks has produced negative responses among white Southerners. The new prominence and upward mobility of black people threatens the social status of numerous whites, particularly among the working classes. "Forget, hell" on the front license plates of revved-up older model cars expresses the genuine sentiments of many who suffer from status anxiety. Of very recent origin is a companion response to black emergence, namely taking offense at what is judged to be arrogance on the part of a people heady with the wine of new pride and self-consciousness.

The moral sense of white people, not surprisingly, is dimmed somewhat by this welter of circumstances. When cultural memory draws to mind, first, the slave status of Negroes, followed by Jim Crow arrangements for interracial living, this image being bloated by the convincing evidence of Negro inferiority, and these factors are joined with the unsettling facts of black competition and black arrogance, the white man's intended good will is easily made ambivalent or diverted. In other words, practical circumstances have militated against any transformation of racial attitudes. Since practical experience is regularly more determinative of one's behavior than his formal ideological (theological) commitments, we need not wonder that the southern value system, with its traditional convictions about the appropriate coexistence of the black and white races, has stifled much of the aspiration to holiness which rightly translates as love of God and neighbor.*

Despite the powerful presence of these social forces, however, we might have expected church teaching to be sufficiently effectual to create tension between the Christian mandate and the accepted racial attitudes of the white

---

*I do not intend here to depreciate the "religious factor." There is ample evidence that the beliefs held by religious people make a difference in their perceptions and behavior; in sociological terms, that religion is an "independent variable." My point is that formal theological propositions are always filtered through cultural experience. In the South, accordingly, the religious factor is not official creeds but what people perceive the church's truth-claims to be, in line with the complex of assumptions and pictures with which cultural participation has equipped them.

South. For the most part, such has not been the case. Instead, the parallel secular and religious currents actually have issued in a reversal of what is from the Christian standpoint the ideal situation. That is, religion has further tightened the hold of racially discriminating convictions, at least that has been the net effect of the churches' influence. What seems to have happened is that religious assumptions deflected moral earnestness. This is ironic and poignant, the more so since few Christians ever have longed with greater passion to build the kingdom of God on earth or been as confident that they were engaged in that enterprise. Perhaps we may account for the disjuncture between intention and accomplishment, in terms common to this analysis, as the churches' failure to see that "Christian teaching" does not exist in a cultural vacuum, that it is always apprehended through the vehicles by which people perceive and communicate.

Theologically speaking, religious assumptions deflect moral earnestness because southern churchmen have been taught that the high God of heaven, who is life's ineluctable reference point, issues a single directive to each person: find forgiveness for your personal sins. This being the divinely imposed, overriding obligation of mankind, consideration of the unloving character of relations between persons, and especially between persons of distinct races, is bound to be depreciated—though not intentionally abrogated. In other words, when religion is defined as status, that is, how one stands before a morally requiring God, it follows that racial concerns will not have more than proximate significance. In recent years, an expanding company of southern ministers and lay leaders have been affirming the unity of black and white under God in church and society —sometimes at their personal peril. Despite their courageous proclamation and example, when the evangelical concern shapes perceptions, this message is viewed as "tacked on," perhaps very important, but neither the central concern nor an organic by-product of the religious life. This is to say, the main practical impact of the churches' message does not penetrate the racial situation of the South. Indeed, in recent years, no doubt as reaction to rapid social change, many ministers have declared that the primacy of evangelism is being eroded by undue attention to economic and racial matters. A number have asserted that what occurs in the marketplace or the county courthouse is only indirectly the business of the church, which is rightly understood as a "spiritual" organization.

This rather curious role of the church, as contributor to the preservation of unloving racial patterns, becomes stranger still when we recall that southern evangelicalism is presented in distinctly moral categories. The Christian life is depicted as a *doing* existence. Note the familiar verbs: one *makes* decision, *remembers* his identity, *practices* what he *preaches*, *bears* witness, *lets* his light *shine*, *wins* the world, *grows* in grace, *gets right* with God. These are hardly metaphors of passivity or complacency. The faithful are continually reminded that it is not enough to "call me Lord, Lord"; such vocation must issue in doing what the Lord says. They believe that the gift of salvation from sin is accompanied by the gift of moral empowerment. Moreover, the basic characterization of God is moral: He has standards, is altogether holy, cannot countenance evil, sends his son to pay the sin-debt, and requires total loyalty. Accordingly, man is defined as moral: one who by (Adam's) choice is alienated, can decide, must decide, and is capable of considerable spiritual attainment. Perhaps this breadth of moral awareness, dominating theology, man's nature, and man's calling, has played into the prevalence of Southerners' sense of moral ambiguity on the racial question. They have handled this awareness, partly by being kind to Negroes as individuals (often in a paternalistic framework), partly by expressing interest in the salvation of the

Negro's soul, and also by the conviction that the reign of justice can be deferred until the divine day of judgment in the world to come.

To summarize this interpretation of the churches' complicity in the hierarchical pattern of racial relations: ultimate confidence of personal redemption deflects the painful ethical question of white supremacy, thus relegating it to secondary importance. In order to do so, an unconventional conception of morality has had to guide the ethical understanding of southern religion. That is, morality is construed in ahistorical categories, for it is associated with *being*, rather than with doing. The rhetoric of doing, so common to southern church life, is actually self-contradictory, since doing, according to this view, consists of *interior* states, resolutions, and convictions. Rhetoric notwithstanding, the principal mode of southern religious sensibilities is not operationally the moral—and no one supposes that it is the aesthetic. In the classical philosophical division, it must then be the ontological. In other words, this form of religious knowledge is delineated by a vivid sense of interiority: one *is* a forgiven sinner; one *hears* God's call; one *knows* he is going to heaven; one *talks* with God in prayer; one *deepens* his devotional life; one *reads* his Bible; one *becomes* the vehicle for the recurrence of all this in the interior lives of others. These are the distinguishing events in the Christian life, as the southern (evangelical) church teaching has it. In standard fashion, it is said that these events, having been drunk to the dregs, *will* bear fruit; we have here a "stages model"—first do this, then that follows. It may be questioned whether human behavior can be so ordered, in the first place. But even assuming that it can be, the habit of mind which generates this form of religious consciousness emanates from a fundamental conviction that the locus of religious reality is "heaven" or "between heaven and earth" or "the interior self." Because history must be defined as "outer" as well as "inner," having to do with public events and relationships, the interpretation is seen to be ahistorical. For, in the final analysis, it views the primal *modus operandi* as being, one *is* a forgiven sinner—and not as doing, one *should love* his neighbor as God loves him.

The preceding treatment of various features in southern church life—the influence of secular factors upon it, the real but limited sense of social responsibility within it, and its essentially ontological or interiorist or privatist modality —has been leading us to the heart of this inquiry into the South's two cultures. Tersely stated, religion is dominantly a conservative or reinforcing agent for the traditional values held by white southern society. Pattern-maintenance has been the primary result, if not the declared intention. Granted, some prophetic activity has taken place. Nevertheless, the overall impact of the church leadership has been priestly in that secular traditions and values have been "baptized" and accorded legitimacy. Usually this happens in line with natural law interpretations. For, articulately or not, white culture has decreed such beliefs as that the Negro's inferior status is in the nature of things, that agrarian or quasi-agrarian society is the most moral type of arrangement for human living, and that the southern churches are the purest in Christendom. In a word, many southern whites have regarded their society as God's most favored. To a greater degree than any other, theirs approximates the ideals the Almighty has in mind for mankind everywhere. Clearly, an attitude of this kind contains few incentives for self-criticism or efforts to redirect southern ways.

In exploring the history of the churches' role as reinforcer of secular traditions, one is struck by the increase in religious expressiveness, of both personal and institutional sorts, which occurred during the period following the Civil War. Anyone familiar with southern history is likely to know that the place of the Christian world view and churches of various denominations was significant much earlier than that, indeed from the very beginning of the colonial era. Never has there been any alternative to Christianity for providing the people with a set of cosmic assumptions. In the early years of the seventeenth century, the Church of England accompanied the American settlers to the New World, to be followed in turn by the institutions of Roman Catholics, Quakers, Congregationalists, Jews, Baptists, Lutherans, Methodists, and numerous other groups later on. Although religious vitality was not the hallmark of the society, there were periodic waves of enthusiasm in 1740-60, the 1780s, 1800-1810, and the 1830s. As we have noted, no rival philosophy ever posed a serious challenge to orthodox Christianity. Moreover religious images and norms informed southern consciousness even for many who were not affiliated with any church. This consensus of the southern population in a single-option religious culture, however, preceded widespread institutional commitment to a religious vision of reality, which did not occur until the period between 1870 and 1930.

Historian C. Vann Woodward describes this phenomenon for the New South era: "Instead of withering away before the advance of industry, science, and urbanization, the Southern legions of Christian soldiers multiplied in numbers and, to judge from appearances, waxed in zeal." In 1890, white church membership figures stood at 6,130,023 while sixteen years later the total was 9,260,899. This amounts to a growth rate of fifty-one percent during a span when population increased by thirty-nine percent.[4] Causation is hard to assess, of course, and any attempt must consider a variety of factors, such as greater population concentration in towns and cities and heightened institutional awareness which accompanied the new complexification of life, as the agrarian mind-set yielded to the urban. Even so, the burgeoning religious statistics are impressive, and call for inquiry into social determinants.

Too often, the emergence of new ideologies (in this case, a theological world view) or the rejuvenation of existing ones is treated cavalierly as the prevalence of a set of social conditions giving rise to a new framework of thinking, whether it be political, economic, religious, or something else. Now there is no use asking if ideologies have social determinants, since of course they do. The aspect of such an inquiry which necessitates greater sophistication is *why* a *particular*, highly specific theology (in our own case) grows from the soil of a given culture. Concretely, we must seek reasons for Evangelical Protestantism—in preference to classical Protestantism, liturgical Protestantism, deism, or Roman Catholicism—becoming the popular religious pattern among white Southerners. Again anthropologist Geertz sheds light. As he sees it, what is at issue is "how . . . ideologies transform sentiment into significance and so make it socially available." [5] For a rationalized system of thought-action to take hold, it must capture the moods, needs, and interests of a substantial sector of the population. A specific interpretation of Christianity becomes dominant for a people when it objectifies both their pains and their self-assertions in its basic symbol structure. By becoming a public universe of discourse it formulates what they prize and what they need to cope with. The process is circular: Social sentiments generate an ideological formulation which in turn attracts people's loyalty by reflecting what they feel deeply, in both positive and negative ways. Continuing, Geertz writes: "It is a confluence of socio-psychological strain and an absence of cultural resources by means of which to make . . . sense of that strain, each exacerbating the other, that sets the stage for the rise of systematic . . . ideologies." [6] "Strain" here must be understood to include anxiety and uncertainty, and "interest" refers to the yearning for power and advantage.

In the nineteenth-century South, there was plenty of "socio-psychological strain." During the period before the

Civil War the dominant white society was caught in an intricate web of ambiguity. After all, slavery was a profound moral contradiction to a people who (like all Americans) had participated in the spirit of liberal democracy. During the last quarter of the eighteenth century, their own kinsmen had been nearly peerless as the architects of national documents which spiritually forbade regarding human beings as property. Moreover, the moral teachings of their Christianity stirred restiveness on the matter of slavery, as did personal friendship with Negroes whom they could relate to appropriately only as beings in their own species.

The role of the clergy in southern society between the Revolution and Reconstruction illuminates the tension existing between the political-religious traditions on the one hand, and the fundamental processes of life in the society on the other.[7] Within the early postrevolutionary generation, the Protestant clergy endeavored to build social cohesion by transforming a scattered, isolated people into community-conscious citizens. With respect to black citizens, they hoped to avoid effective differentiation by including both races in a single social arrangement. For complicated reasons they failed in this ambition, and compromised by working to save the souls of individual Negroes.

For the clergy who flourished in the 1830s and 1840s the primary accomplishment was the formation of denominational solidarity, even regional separateness, by the three largest groups. In helping construct southern Methodist, southern Baptist, and southern Presbyterian organizations, they were leading the masses toward a sense of identification with an intermediate collectivity, a group larger in size than the local congregation or community, but smaller than the total society. The effect of this was the development of a social image by which white Southerners saw themselves in corporate terms; here we witness a major, if unwitting, contribution of religion to secular society, specifically, to the crystallization of the Solid South image and the powerful self-consciousness of the Southern Baptist Convention. Of great significance is the fact that during these two decades clergymen moved into a central role in the society, as educators, guardians of the collective life, and models of the good life for the privileged. Perhaps more than any other vocational group they were effective in promoting social integration.

Over the last fifteen years before the Civil War, southern ministers developed a proslavery argument. As the one strategic elite for the entire society, they attempted to integrate it on the basis of a moral philosophy of public responsibility. This is not to suggest that they were "clean" in their support of slavery, however. Rather, it had now fallen their lot to hold the (white) society together, to sanctify its ways, and to generate *elan* for its causes, so that approval of slavery would be automatic and casual. They perceived that its demise would spell the doom of southern ways.

There was continuity between the place of the church before the war and its role after 1865. Yet because conditions had been altered so dramatically, the exact function was different. Following Reconstruction, the institutional life of the churches really flowered in that, as we have noted, they grew in numbers, size, and fervor. The new factor appears to have been the sense that one had a societal obligation to belong to the church. Whereas in antebellum days, the clergy were the foundation of social coherence, now the whole population must perform that function. Mass solidarity was required for the legitimation of an entire society.[8] Accordingly in the postwar era, the elite was broadened to include every (white) person.

Religion's coming to the fore as a conspicuous and indispensable quality in southern life served a number of social and psychological functions for a defeated, disorganized, and poverty-stricken people. In terms of "strain theory," it helped them cope with the anguish of social-psychological disequilibrium and afforded them a measure of conquest over anxiety. And we must highlight the salient fact that it was a particular form of Christianity, Evangelical Protestantism, which flourished. The denominations embodying this outlook had become parochially southern owing to schism from their respective national bodies before the war, as we have seen. Following Reconstruction these communions, especially the Methodist and Baptist, presented themselves attractively to the populace. This was due in part to their being organizations whose leaders and membership were confined to the southern region. But more than this, their approaches to theology, ethics, and churchmanship struck a responsive chord within southern sensibilities.

Southern whites had lived with feelings of guilt for a long time. Many slaveholders viewed their economic-social system with ambivalence. In this context, Evangelical preachments struck home by virtue of the emphasis on man's propensity for breaking the law of God. But once his deep moral disquietude (with some traces of masochism) had been sated by vivid reiteration, the churchgoer experienced relief. He was told that forgiveness is a *state* which one enters upon conversion. This recognition enabled him to ignore his society's complicity in discriminating between races because he could relegate moral questions to the periphery. According to the message he heard, the Christian is merely a sojourner in this world; evils have to be endured, and the evangelical gospel makes them endurable. Ironically, many southern whites got relief from the guilt of perpetuating an immoral social-economic system by subscribing to the tenets of a guilt-oriented theology. Such hymns as "The Old Rugged Cross," "Nothing but the Blood," and "Blessed Assurance" possessed deeper meaning than most perceived.

In connection with "interest theory," evangelical Christianity communicated to southern whites some sense of power. Since the end of Reconstruction, acquisition of power has been a particular temptation to a people beset by inferiority feelings and stung by criticisms from outside —a factor which may partially explain the southern infatuation with championship football teams and beauty contests, and Southerners' brashness in making claims for the superiority of regional social amenities. In tapping this aspect of southern consciousness we are probing the powerful appeal of a religious interpretation which exalts eternal spiritual victory. Whether or not this comes through a memorable single experience, it carries unassailable interior knowledge. Existential conquest, indeed even the capacity for controlling the circumstances of one's life, has escaped many citizens because of the region's poverty and isolation. But religious victory, in this simplistic form, has been within reach and becomes for many a *fait accompli*. Only Evangelical Protestantism from among all the families of Christianity provides so grandiose a promise of assurance.

In addition, religion has delivered the consolation of *ultimate* advantage, at both personal and denominational levels. Many a sermon has magnified texts like, "If God be for us who can be against us?" the sentiment being that though worldly conditions may be oppressive, the heavenly home awaits. Small wonder that much popular hymnology has pointed to dependent trust, faithful waiting, and the promise of sweetness in the by-and-by. One is inclined to associate the popular Baptist stress on the "eternal security of the believer" with this psycho-social need, and similarly the Methodist confidence, reached by a different means but achieving the same goal, that reclamation by grace may occur repeatedly. As far as denominational issues are concerned, we can only be impressed by the self-consciousness and immodesty of the southern bodies. From Reconstruction forward, ecclesiastics compared the religious situation of the South with that prevailing elsewhere—itself a revealing disposition and always to the South's advantage.

From many quarters came assessments of the superior purity of regional Methodism, Presbyterianism, or Baptist life, with the implication or even the assertion that their brand was the hope of the world.*

Important as these factors are in pointing to the solid appeal of Evangelical Protestantism to southern whites, in my judgment they stop short of the most telling component in the linkage between church and culture. For, beyond enabling them to cope with strain, stake out their superiority, and assuage their guilt, both as souls before God and as crisis-ridden society, religion legitimated the (white) Southern Way of Life. What was most fundamental to the experience of the people was Southernness, not religious faith, truth, or integrity as such. Everything, the unfinished business of the society, the primary issue in their shared memory, the matters of most vital concern, focused upon the legitimation of a way of life. Public and private health were dependent upon absolution from guilt over the most serious departure in history from the nation's moral tradition, and the restoration of its sense of self-esteem. This deep-going need was met in numerous ways, including the ebulliency of "New South" plans for turning the region's God-given superiority into a magnificent civilizational accomplishment.** But given the South's

*One is reminded here of the sentiments expressed by a pastor in the Southern Baptist Convention at the annual session in Denver, 1970, incident upon a debate over the convention press's proposed publication of a more liberal Bible commentary. He warned that "we're going to be one of the has-been churches" if the Southern Baptists veer toward liberalism. The feeling, "we're the only ones left," is neither new nor fading.

** Paul M. Gaston has written most perceptively of the role of the New South myth as a foil to Reconstruction, populism, and, later, exposures of the faltering socio-economic system. He argues history and actual resources, the route *par excellence* was bound to be spiritual, combining moral, affective, and metaphysical aspects. The popular version of Christianity supplied the palliative.

For this analysis the sociological theory of Emile Durkheim seems unusually pertinent.[9] As Durkheim viewed religion, it has intimate connection with society. This is true on two primary levels. First, the social environment of life, which is as objective a framework as the physical environment, is actually the source of men's identity, protection, provision, and opportunity. Second, belief-system, moral position, and ritual acts are closely correlated with the general structure of the society. In simpler terms, this interpretation of religion and society argues that what people think of as God, a transcendent personal being, is in fact society, the context in which we experience, are shaped, have interaction, and so on. Whether or not all the theological implications of this theory of religion are accepted, it sheds much light upon the relation between religion and society in the American South. For southern society is, dramatically, not merely contextually, an objective reality, a psychosocial entity, a moral community, the embodiment of heritage, a shared memory, or a "state of mind." There is something of a collective consciousness imbedded in the region's citizens.

Tying this in with a previous discussion, we are now ready to assert that the South, or Southernness, because of the intensity with which people practice it owing to defensiveness, guilt, defeat, and isolation, is itself a kind of cultural system. To say this is to go beyond describing

---

that the myth was tenacious, exhibiting usefulness for several generations, because interest groups opposed to change manipulated it as an instrument of their own purposes. See *The New South Creed* (New York: Alfred A. Knopf, 1970), pp. 219-25.

it as merely a culture. The concept of system adds the qualities of rationality, coherence, consciousness, and order to culture which is relatively accidental and one-dimensional. Let us apply Geertz's definition of culture to South and Southernness: "an historically transmitted pattern of meanings embodied in symbols, a system of inherited conceptions expressed in symbolic forms by means of which men communicate, perpetuate, and develop their knowledge about and attitudes toward life." (See p. 18, above.) Now, raising that to a systemic power, we observe that those meanings, conceptions, and symbols are given the properties of constraint and transcendence. Stated simply, southern mores are accorded a certain divine quality. They are not only the way things are, they are the way things should be. Perhaps only by this exponential activity could white Southerners have tolerated themselves in the midst of a time-space which valued, in addition, democratic ideals and industrial progress.

Consider some of the elements comprising the (white) Southern Way of Life: the Confederate flag; "Dixie"; distinctive speech accents; regional foods and culinary styles; the sense of regional apartness and superiority; specifiable convictions about the appropriate relations between the races; the same about the role of women; the notion that trade unions are both unnecessary and conspiratorial; belief that all social disputes can be resolved through personal diplomacy; *Gemeinschaft* assumptions about human collectivities, including cities; a preference for personality extroversion; the tendency to identify "American" as Anglo-Saxon; pride in agrarian or small-town manners; etc.

I am suggesting that to a peculiarly intense degree Southernness as a cultural system provides the framework for living, complete with metaphysical claims (unformulated) and moral constraints. Whereas the resident of Kansas or Wisconsin, for example, also lives in a culture with eminently visible patterns, typically he has not felt the need

45

to construct a defense of it and invest it with some kind
of ultimate sanction—to create a Midwest mythology. The
relatively greater ease with which one moves from Midwest
to another culture than has been true of the mobile
Southerner is some indication of the point being made.
At least until recently it was no more possible to forget
that one is a Southerner than for the Jew to have a comparable lapse of memory. It is this regional-historical cultural system by which southern people have identified
themselves, which they have defended, which they have
carried as baggage wherever they go, which many have
sought to spread as an evangel. For millions, most having
few opportunities to compare or proselytize, Southernness
has been the ultimate social good news. In a descriptive
sense, society is God.

What is at issue here is another form of the paradox
which wends its way through this entire essay. Here the
form is not, how can Christian identity and racism co-
exist, but rather its cultic projection, how can one belong
to two moral communities, church and South? Potential
conflict is aroused by the fact that the Christian Church
demands a total loyalty, while the South as a cultural
system presents itself as a nurturing and teaching agency
lacking in self-critical powers. In very different ways both
Christianity and Southernness lay exclusive claim upon
the white people of the region.

Does it follow that southern men and women practice
duplicity or betrayal? What of the millions of them who
intend to profess faith in religion's deity, the God of Abra-
ham, Isaac, and Jacob, and of Jesus Christ, in the setting of
Christian theism? To the query, are they merely deceiving
themselves, I think we must reply "no," in a great many
cases. Rather, they are participants in *two* primary frameworks of meaning, two cultural systems. Their lives are
governed by two culture-ethics, God who is society and
God who is the subject of existential experience within

the Christian community. *Both* provide context, identity, community, and moral constraint.

Actually this dual allegiance, if pursued circumspectly, need not falsify or abominate the religious intensity of the southern devout. Although central and left-wing (the South's kind) Protestant theory guards scrupulously against the worship of state or culture, or uncritical loyalty to either, the reality of human life is that men live in polypolitan cultures, the commercial, political, professional, familial, religious, biophysical, psychodynamic, and so on. Nor is there, according to my assessment, any compelling reason why the Christian should counterpose loyalty in the religious city to other agents of context and value. If he does and must owe other allegiances, and if all of the realms are affirmed to be arenas of God's concern and direction, fastidious differentiation between the two cultures is barely appropriate. I concur in a recent statement of this position, that interdependence rather than dominance rightly characterizes the relationship between the various "cities" of man's life.[10]

Nevertheless, there must be some continuity, some rationalized pattern of interdependence, an element of compatibility, if excessive and pathological loyalties (including the religious) are to be avoided. It is also imperative, with reference to religious faith, that avenues be found for preserving integrity of belief, commitment, and morality. Surely there are certain attitudes and patterns of behavior which are acceptable in other "cities" but which are intolerable for Christians, no matter how necessary and potentially constructive may be citizenship in those many cities.

Only when the question is posed in this way does the southern Christian find himself on the brink of violating integrity. Because his regional culture carries the weight of a mythology—a sacralized framework of meaning—and a cultural *system*—a rationalized and coherent milieu, he is in a morally awkward position. To make matters worse, this coherent cultural system has as a major constitutive element a fundamental conviction about white supremacy and racial discrimination. For we are dealing with moral views on race which constitute the distinctive value of Southernness; no other widespread cultural feature so separates the South from the rest of the nation and the modern world. And this is precisely the problem since, on any rendering of Christianity which is historically accurate and discerning, love of God and neighbor are self-evidently its definitive norm and virtues. After making generous allowances for diversity within the Christian tradition, one finally concludes that it teaches absolutely that all human groups and individuals are to be judged as human, not as members of a racial or national group, or as accomplished, or as unlettered, or by association with any phenomenal quality. In theological language, persons are to be assessed by virtue of their being granted inherent worth and capacity in the divine purpose. So there *is* an essential contradiction between regionality and religion with respect to *this* primary value. Consequently, citizenship in the earthly city of culture would seem to have taken moral precedence over membership in the kingdom of God.

Earlier we have considered several avenues of explanation for the essentially conservative impact of religion despite the centrality of the love dynamic in its teaching. Now it is time to inquire into the curious fact that versions of Christianity which highlighted the application of its love ethic to social problems and were the leading edge in mainline American Protestantism from the 1890s to the 1930s made only the slightest impact upon the churches in the South. During the period when Walter Rauschenbusch, Washington Gladden, other clergymen, and the major leadership of the Federal Council of the Churches of Christ in America were promoting vigorous programs of Christian social ministry, the southern churches were reaching out almost exclusively to the salvation of souls, with ministry understood individualistically. There were exceptions, to be sure, especially in the first twenty years of this century, but these were limited largely to visionary denominational officials and local clerics.[11] They seem never to have animated either the rank and file of churchmen or formal ecclesiastical policy and priorities. Moreover once the era of the 1920s had set in, retrenchment in the older evangelical patterns was the dominant mood. The period 1890-1930 witnessed the first sharply divergent courses between churches North and South in American religious history. Before the Civil War, northern influence on southern church leadership was continual and significant, and parallels obtained for the following twenty to thirty years. But once the social gospel orientation emerged, the two geographical areas were to go their separate ways with a vengeance. We must ask why this development occurred when it did.

For what reasons did the social gospel fail to evoke popular support from southern whites? The explanations usually offered include: Evangelical Protestantism is not morphologically structured in such a way as to accommodate a social ethic (a position taken and defended earlier in this chapter); or, the ecclesiastical establishment has been defensive of regional mores, racial and otherwise; or, social-gospel movements were spawned in the North by theological liberals, hence were tainted by association. Perhaps these are superficial, however, neglecting to take into account the real character of Southernness as a cultural system-mythology operating as the model for living.

Based on the analysis that religion and regionality are both primary frameworks of meaning for white southern people with regionality predominant in the practical ordering of life, any semblance of a social-gospel ideology would have upset the balance and rendered impossible mutual support between church and culture. The South's particular compound for the formation of Christendom would thereby have been destroyed. Any novel interpretation of the Christian world view with intense focus on the relation of ethical values to social conditions would have constituted a formidable threat to the (white) Southern Way of Life. In the process of challenging, then overturning, traditional social patterns, especially racial, it would have wrought disruption. Southernness, the "God above God," would have been dethroned, and supports crumbled.

Stated baldly, if the social gospel or any kin position, had taken root in southern consciousness, a profound *secular* assault would have been mounted against the South's delicate balance. This is not merely a *theological* disturbance and new departure, but a basic challenge to a people's sacralized life-style. The South's penchant for making myths, reflected as plantation elegance and New South progress, among others, extended also to the religious realm. Here it took the form of self-defense as self-recommendation in some such rhetoric as "we have the most righteous people, the friendliest society, and the purest churches anywhere." This religious mythology served as a foil against incursions from ethical liberalism based in the North. But it was more necessary than secular myths, I contend, because it both assuaged deep-going guilt and stamped the divine seal of approval upon a culture in urgent need of legitimation. Whatever fortifications might be required, the social gospel must be kept out.

This being the case, church personnel who have called Christian congregations to take the lead for the transformation of assumptions, structures, and goals in existing *secular* society contend with forces other and more powerful than theological conservatism, or simple inertia. A certain *religious* strategy, if successfully carried out, would transform the sacralized secular society, and that would indeed be a dramatic achievement. The people of the churches, by their lights, have acted wisely and well in steadfastly resisting the encroachments of socially oriented Christianity, for they have rightly, if inchoately, discerned its revolutionary potential. The slogan "keep Alabama as you have known it," which appeared on posters urging Alabamians to elect George C. Wallace as governor in 1970, reflects a profound layer of sentiment running throughout southern experience. Novel *religious* interpretations would certainly have played havoc with the retention of traditionalism by preventing Southerners from keeping their homeland as they knew it.

This way of construing the dynamics of southern culture seems to illuminate several religious or quasi-religious features which attract a large clientele. For example, the number and strength of Masonic lodges in the region's communities indicates some of the currents which flow beneath the surface. (This topic invites research not yet undertaken.) Without as yet having embarked on a systematic study of their significance, I infer that these para-religious brotherhoods function as further reinforcement to the two independent frameworks of meaning, regionality and religion. One senses that for many grass-roots Southerners, investing one's self in the ritual, fellowship, and social service of the lodge is perceived as a highly patriotic act. Moreover it is inconceivable that criticism of the traditional culture or of religious orthodoxy could emanate from these sanctuaries.

Remarkably similar in constituency and outlook, one suspects, is the "men's Bible class" which meets in hundreds of church buildings, especially those belonging to the popular denominations. Often spectacularly large and cult-like, being built around the personality of a veteran teacher, usually a dynamic figure in the business community, these classes tend to operate independently of the church which quarters them. (Curiously, the institution takes credit for them in its statistics, while often finding their presence troublesome.) It dare not suggest an alternative ritual, or seek to appoint the teacher, or determine the literature to be used. Procedurally, the men's Bible class is very nearly as esoteric as the Masonic lodge. Furthermore, it is as about as unlikely as the lodge to offer a critical word toward the culture, religious orthodoxy, or the secular status quo. The church's minister upstairs might feint toward a socially prophetic judgment and get by with it, but hardly the class teacher. Perhaps—I do mean "perhaps" in the absence of conclusive data—these two groups (both male in makeup, it should be noted) which are not composed of red-necks as a usual thing, have the appeal to the middle classes, the accepted people, that the Ku Klux Klan and the White Citizens' Councils possess for the lower classes, those who are alienated. This appears to be the case especially with reference to our issue of societal reinforcement. The methods differ—the middle class does not use overtly hostile tactics, but the goals are comparable. Inside the sacred walls may be found not only identity and community but also a tacit means to legitimate the cultural heritage and the existing values. Both serve to preserve, and both use religious symbols and associations to that end.

Resorting now to sheer speculation, I wonder if something of the same cultural pressure may not operate subtly in the South's almost frenetic preoccupation with the prohibition cause. Is it possible that the intense, well-organized crusades against the sale and use of alcoholic beverages and liquor-by-the-drink provisions reflect more than moral or religious concerns? A partial answer lies in the tendency to lay many of society's evils at the feet of alcoholic usage, which is surely a dodge from something. It is remarkable how general has been the view that if society could be rid of demonic drink many of its ills, of all sorts, would be cured. Perhaps another image has been operative, namely, the concern that the southern *modus vivendi* would be shifted away from its agrarian or small-town, family-centered, and intimate social arrangement if bars and lounges were to become a primary context for socializing. Conversing over a beer or highball would be distinctly different from swapping tales over coffee or a Co-Cola (sic), and would symbolize significant social change.

In his important book about the putative religious revival in America during the Eisenhower years, Will Herberg argued that the situation confronting immigrants, "the uprooted," afforded the background for that surge in religious interest.[12] Especially among the third-generation foreign-born was church or synagogue affiliation necessary because religion alone met the dual criteria of being acceptably American and facilitating membership in middle-sized human collectivities. Being culturally encouraged to forsake association with the hyphenated communities, Italian-American, Polish-American, and so on, in the interest of unassailable patriotism, they turned to the churches both to take the place of those suspect associations and to achieve identification with the American mainstream. Under such conditions, religious affiliation was useful for coming into a sense of social belonging. Neither Herberg's written exposition nor his personal comments purport to deal with the South, however, since the social psychology of immigrant life has never been more than a marginal part of regional experience. Southerners have not had to turn to church or synagogue for small-group identification, even though the social perquisites of church fellowship have been widely distributed. Until recently at least, this feature of mental health has been built into the very structure of a *Gemeinschaft* society.

Nevertheless, the white people of the South, like northern immigrants and their neighbors, have been pressured by social cricumstances into religious identification. Down South, there has been a *societal obligation* to belong. That is, pursuing the logic of this essay's central contention, regional citizens who abstain from lining themselves up with the church fail to ratify the churches' ultimate legitimation of the southern heritage and culture system, leaving room for the judgment that the South may in fact bear massive corporate guilt or to be inferior in its attainments. The pressure upon every last citizen to affiliate is heavy, often compulsive, so much so that there would appear to be other incentives than the evangelical. Cultural forces give the unchurched person the impression that he is somehow a threat to the entire society, a traitor to the cause, an inauthentic member of the regional community. Accordingly, the white Southerner must belong to the church for the sake of establishing the solidarity and legitimacy of his culture. It follows that the churches are shielded from being prophetic, for any affirmation or testimony which serves to impede or make difficult the act of affiliating would amount to a disruption of the Southern Way of Life.

Bringing these observations about the South's two cultures, regionality and religiosity, into the present, we may observe what effect the decline in regional self-consciousness, particularly among the young and more cosmopolitan, is likely to have upon the place of the church in southern society. As Southernness becomes less important, uncritical subscription and loyalty to church religion is apt to follow a parallel course. This constitutes the crisis of the southern churches in the early 1970s. What is not clear at this juncture is whether the churches can tie their attractiveness to other features of life than the reinforcement and legitimation of the traditional (white) Southern Way of Life, and thereby preserve for their ministry a constructive role in the society.

NOTES

1. Merton L. Dillon, "Religion in Lubbock," in *A History of Lubbock*, pt. 3, ed. Lawrence L. Graves (Lubbock: West Texas Museum Association, 1961), pp. 449-516.

2. Avery O. Craven, *An Historian and the Civil War* (Chicago: University of Chicago Press, 1964), chap. 12.

3. Dillon, "Lubbock," pp. 456-57.

4. C. Vann Woodward, *Origins of the New South, 1877-1913* (Baton Rouge: Louisiana State University Press, 1951), pp. 448-49.

5. Clifford Geertz, "Ideology as a Cultural System," in *Ideology and Discontent,* ed. David E. Apter (Glencoe: Free Press, 1964), pp. 56-57.

6. *Ibid.,* p. 64.

7. In the discussion of this point, I am heavily indebted to an unpublished paper, "The Southern Clergy as a Strategic Elite: 1780-1870," presented by Donald G. Mathews to the American Historical Association, December, 1970.

8. The same concern is illustrated by the career of Booker T. Washington. In the words of one interpreter, Washington's invitation to dinner with President Roosevelt in the fall of 1901 caused much adverse comment because among "white Southerners the entertainment of a Negro at the White House, even though he was Booker T. Washington, was an implied threat to the continuance of segregation." This kind of reaction was due to a new social context in the South in that during the 1890s leadership was passing "from the paternalistic former slaveholders to the anti-Negro lower-class whites." Samuel R. Spencer, Jr., *Booker T. Washington and the Negro's Place in American Life* (Boston: Little, Brown, 1955), pp. 132-33, 103.

9. See Emile Durkheim, *The Elementary Forms of the Religious Life* (New York: Collier, 1961), pp. 235-50, *passim.*

10. See William Clebsch, *From Sacred to Profane America* (New York: Harper, 1968), chap. 7.

11. For indication or argumentation that the social gospel did move South, see the following. E. Charles Chatsfield, "The Southern Sociological Congress: Organization of Uplift,"

Tennessee Historical Quarterly XIX (December, 1960), 328–47; Chatsfield, "The Southern Sociological Congress: Rationale of Uplift," *Tennessee Historical Quarterly* XX (March, 1961), 51-64. John Lee Eighmy, *Churches in Cultural Captivity*, a forthcoming publication from the University of Tennessee Press. Wayne Flynt, "Dissent in Zion: Alabama Baptists and Social Issues, 1900-1914," *Journal of Southern History* XXXV (November, 1969), 523-42. Robert Moats Miller, "Fourteen Points on the Social Gospel in the South," *Southern Humanities Review* I (Summer, 1967), 126-40.

12. Will Herberg, *Protestant, Catholic, Jew* (Garden City: Doubleday, 1960).

3
GOD AND THE SOUTHERN PLANTATION SYSTEM

I

I believe it was Uncle Remus who told the little boy who listened to his nightly stories that experience is what you get when you don't listen to your ma and pa. It also is what you get when you go outside other authorities such as books. There comes a time when the thoughts of probably every social scientist who is immersed in his subject take a personal turn; when he distinguishes between his life experience and his study experiences and undertakes to determine what each has contributed to the other. This essay will attempt to put the facts of my own experiences and observations, widened and deepened by the literature, into a context which, for me, illuminates the nature and meaning of religion in the South.

I well remember the old Methodist church I rather reluctantly but regularly attended when I was growing up on a plantation in South Carolina. Founded by Bishop Francis Asbury long before the War Between the States, it still stands, though services no longer are held in it. One of the thousands of abandoned or dying rural churches in the United States it, like most of the others, fell before good roads and automobiles, but its general spirit and outlook were transplanted to the nearby town center.

Southern town and even city churches generally might almost be described as transplanted rural institutions. The old church I knew was once a flourishing thing attended by the gentry and their hangers-on of the community who in the hush of every Sunday morning had nothing else to do except wait for church. Before the war the slaves of the planters sat in the gallery. The dead of the gentry, once buried on individual plantations, later were laid to rest in the cemetery surrounding the church where their poorer relatives and even family pets also were buried. Some of the pets were black servants. The size and quality of the stone monuments marked the degree of affluence, or lack of it, of the ones buried beneath them, an index of the community's status hierarchy.

A succession of ministers lived with their families in the parsonage nearby. The minister was not the only one who chastised us for our sins, but it was he who was expected, licensed, and even paid to do so. It was difficult for him to be "one of the boys" but occasionally one came along who could unbend enough to be called "our kind of preacher." The annual revival during the cotton lay-by season marked the high point of the minister's efforts. Ill provided with public amusements, except for Saturday night brawls during this season of general idleness, the revival normally enjoyed great success. Periodically the minister sought through regular and special collections from the congregation to raise money for his own salary and to help support the denomination's missionaries abroad. The good men of the congregation, but more especially the devout women who formed masculine-approved missionary societies, generously supported this cause even though, before the War Between the States, it might be necessary to sell a slave or so in order to do so. Or so the scoffers sometimes unfeelingly said. The minister rarely if ever had anything to say about child labor, sharecropping, illiteracy, or race relations. I had known child laborers, sharecroppers, and illiterates, white and black, all my life but I did not know the condition of these people constituted social problems until I was well along in college. We heard much, however, about the evils of dancing, card-playing, and the consumption of alcoholic beverages. It was only after the relative loss of control over Negroes incident to their mass emancipation from slavery that the Methodists particularly became concerned about the dangers of strong drink.

The mood of the community generally was one of piety if we think of this word as involving the sharing and the orientation of experience. Piety has to do with personal support of that system of traditional values and sentiments appropriate to the requirements of a situation. It is, as Kenneth Burke epigrammatically puts it, "the sense of what properly goes with what." [1] In my case, and in the case of thousands of other Southerners, it was an experience which went well beyond my life upon the immediate plantation where I grew up and the church I attended. It was, in addition, an experience with a system of society, a plantation system, including all the institutions in that system. In it I was located and knew who I was supposed to be and what I was expected to do and to think. Of course, like many others, I took the system and the situation in which it operated for granted but now I propose to try to make sense of it, to "size up the situation," as we say.

Of course, my effort in this brief chapter will be incomplete, but it may serve to show the context in which the southern church and its religion should, I think, be understood.

II

Whether economic or cultural factors predominate in shaping the institutions of a given social order it is certain there is a strain toward consistency in the relations between them. The institutions of no society are transplanted without adaptation to another environment if they survive at all. Either the transplanted institutions transform the habitat, or the new habitat transforms them, or both are changed as they interact with each other. In any case, the result is the creation of a new and different "situation" which has to be analyzed in terms of the constituent interacting factors which produce and maintain it. I am concerned here with a certain constellation of factors and institutions, among them the church and the religion associated with it, which have defined the situation and which we have termed "the South."

I am considering the church and religion in the South as developing in response to a situational imperative apart from any judgment, good or bad, we may be tempted to pass upon it. Our conservatives or fundamentalists have pronounced religion in the South the best to be found anywhere[2] whereas our liberals or modernists have found it to be woefully inadequate and superstitious, but a rearward look suggests that the development of religion in the South, regardless of ethnic, denominational, or ecclesiastical differences, was and is the unintended result of the immediate intentions of many generations of men. No individual or group of individuals sought to make it what it finally became nor what it is becoming. It developed from situational factors and changes in these factors that lie at least in part outside human plan and purpose.[3]

Many observers of both liberal and conservative persuasion have commented upon the unique character of religious phenomena in the South. Kenneth Bailey has sketched this character and described the South at the turn of the twentieth century as "a land of piety and tradition" preoccupied "with individual repentance, a dogged insistence on Biblical inerrancy, a tendency toward overt expression of intense religious emotions: these legacies of frontier revivalism still held a primacy."[4] Of course, there were individual and local exceptions to the "almost single-minded emphasis upon individual regeneration," and of course peoples and areas outside the homogeneous South often exhibited very much the same emphasis, but the rise and spread of the social gospel with its compassion for depressed classes, its doctrinal unorthodoxy, its rational criticism, and its involvement in political movements looking to the elimination of social inequities was far more prevalent in the religious behavior of the heterogeneous and urban North and West.

Religion in the South began as an Old-World transplant, went through various modifying stages during the westward frontier expansion, and in the course of time acquired an institutional character implying constitution, stability, and tradition, and was reabsorbed with considerable modifications into preexisting ecclesiastical structures which, incident to the slavery controversy and the Civil War, separated from their northern counterparts. Belief-systems and institutional dogmas took deep root in an overwhelmingly rural society of planters, white and Negro peasants and squatters, and yeoman farmers. The cost of maintaining the more or less formal institutional structures was paid for by returns from various commercial staples such as cotton, tobacco, sugarcane, and lesser crops. The cost was returned in full measure by the moral support which the religious belief-system gave to the agricultural system at the center of which was the plantation.

Among the Protestant denominations various sorts of Baptists, the folk-church of the white South, seem to have become more "southern" than those of other denominations and the Quakers least so, but all these denominations were but minor variations from common points of cultural assumptions. The tradition which they shared and supported raised an infallible Bible, and especially the King James Version of it, to the position which had been occupied by an infallible Pope leading cynics such as H. L. Mencken to characterize the South as the Bible Belt.[5] Even beneath the surface differences between those variations from white Protestantism represented by Catholicism, Judaism, and Negro Christianity there were and are common values, assumptions, and other intangibles which comprise that indefinable thing called the Southern Way of Life. Of course, there were important doctrinal and behavioral differences between Protestantism, Catholicism, and Judaism in the South as in other parts of the nation, and as the common southern culture underlying them developed and strengthened Southerners become more conscious of the differences that remained and more convinced that they were greater than actually was the case. There were ministerial and political politicians who clung to the differences and made a profession of advertising and manipulating them. Protestant hostility toward Judaism and Catholicism intensified, and suspicion grew among whites generally that Negro Christianity was spurious. But religious orthodoxy, a sort of fossilized piety, was at the core of southern cultural orthodoxy which, when challenged by scientific and theological advances, was consciously and defensively formulated, especially in white Protestantism, into what came to be called fundamentalism. Fundamentalism in the United States has had its greatest strength in the rural areas of the South.

III

But what is the South, the situation in which I propose that we try to understand its church and its religion? It is not simply the South of the census nor even of that geographical area which appears at the bottom of the map. I think we do not get at the nature or essence of the South by adding up the geographies and the histories of the political divisions which various authorities have called "southern states." The South is not a state, nor any one of the states, nor any combination of states. The history of North Carolina is not a chapter in the history of the South.

The South is not recognized in the Constitution of the United States. Yet we have a name for it, and we talk about it as if it were an objective entity, as if it exists. At least on one occasion its people engaged in a collective enterprise when it waged war against a common enemy. As a result its members spoke of themselves as "we Southerners" set off in opposition to others referred to by General Lee as "those people." Yet when we have stripped away that which is common to all humanity, to the people of the Western world, to rural and agricultural people everywhere, to people who live in interracial situations, and to the people of the United States generally, what we have left, or some part of what we have left, is the South. But by that time the society is substantially rather thin amounting to little more than an abstraction or an idea. It was and is, however, an idea deemed significant because people both inside and outside the society chose to look at it significantly and to search for and to magnify differences both real and imagined. It was an idea originally laid down upon a territory whose boundaries were very indistinct. Today they are even more indistinct as the obvious uniformity of urban life steadily emancipates the South from its old territorial locus.

Significant or not there have been and are real differences between the South and the rest of the nation. In the context of the nation as a whole the South is stigmatized as an area of pervasive poverty especially since President Franklin Roosevelt characterized it as the nation's Economic Problem No. 1. More recently it has received widespread notice in connection with President's Johnson's antipoverty program. After the War Between the States its political solidarity gained for the region the name of Solid South. Religious orthodoxy, poverty, and political conservatism are the three sets of factors which consistently appear together in each of the "Souths" of the world listed by Seymour Martin Lipset. Others mentioned are southern Italy, Quebec in

Canada, the Scottish Highlands of Great Britain, western Norway in addition to the American South. It has been said that "every country has a South"—a social if not a geographical South. In these "relatively poor and economically less developed regions" citizens regularly vote conservative even when their own best interests would appear to dictate otherwise. The minds of the people, Lipset goes on to say, "are dominated by 'traditionalistic' values."

In these areas the social structure remains in some part the way it was before the age of capitalism and the free-market economy. The positions of rich and poor are defined as the natural order of things and are supported by personal, family, and local loyalties rather than viewed as a product of impersonal economic and social forces, subject to change through political action. At the same time the poor peasant or worker performs a role which has an obvious meaning and value, and he derives gratification from stable personal relationships and ceremonial activities embracing the whole community. Religious belief tends to be strong and to support the *status quo*.[6]

IV

The gross factors of economics, politics, and religion in the general situation as represented by these various "Souths" may show similarities, but when we come to probe their historical and social roots considerations more or less special to each have to be taken into account. Of particular importance in understanding the American South is the longtime presence in it of the plantation institution. The plantation was never present in the Scottish Highlands, but it does appear to have been the central fact in the determination and history of the American South. Let me outline some of its more salient features.

Since Columbus the New World has received or spawned a large number of movements, enterprises, and organizations most of which failed to catch on and subsequently died. The effort to transplant the English manor to Maryland and elsewhere failed, but an enterprise directed toward the exploitation of virtually free land to produce agricultural staples for the European market which took form in various parts of Latin America, the West Indies, and the American South succeeded, spread, and came to be called the plantation. In the American South this institution—which must be distinguished from settlements called by the same name in New England—came by 1860 to occupy favorable lands from Maryland to eastern Texas or wherever it could get its staples down to the ocean at low cost. From the West Indies it was transplanted to South Carolina and to Louisiana, but in Virginia and Maryland it began an independent development as profit from the cultivation of tobacco began to be realized.

The reduction of vast forests and the cultivation of land almost free for the taking in the American Southeast required a great output of labor, beyond the ability of European families such as there were, to supply. In the situation there was considerably more land capable of producing marketable staples than there was labor to till it. Recourse was first had to white indentured labor from Europe and later to Negro slaves from Africa. Thus what we have to observe getting under way in the very early days of this area are a number of small single-purpose enterprises each mobilizing a varying number of nondescript people to act together to clear away the trees and to produce a crop for which there promises to be a market and a profit. The single plantation is a loose collectivity somewhere out there on the moving frontier proximate to a navigable stream or river and later to a dirt road or railroad. Like every crescive institution anywhere, it begins with collective activity and a purpose which dominates the program of its leader or planter, but, as Everett Hughes has taught us, there is always some unfinished business.[7] From one generation to the next, there is always the problem of getting and controlling labor for ends outside the interests and wishes of those who are controlled. It was when these activities assumed a structure and became routine to the extent that plans for the future had to be made that the plantation as an institution can be said to have been accomplished. As it adapted its members to its own purpose and as people began to depend upon it, it became part of the accepted and natural order of things. Its head man, the planter, gained in practical economic and political importance as over against the ordinary trader and farmer, a fact sensed by himself and by the rest of the people. A family dynasty could be established as the son of the planter followed in the manner of the father. As a cross between farmers and knights, planters pursued a sort of military agriculture for which they thought it necessary to mold those who worked for them in the fields into good slaves or sharecroppers. The church and its religion fell into line to teach servants that they not only had to but should obey their masters. Thus the authority of the plantation came naturally to divide men into subordinates and superordinates as the institution moved along the southern frontier from Maryland to eastern Texas.

The plantation institution appeared in other parts of the New World but what is of major importance about the southern plantation is that it was the first frontier-created institution to take root and survive in this particular environment to overshadow those transplanted, however much modified, from abroad. In New England the transplanted church was to assume an unchallenged authority in relation to other institutions, which continued until the days of Channing and Emerson and even much later. In the South, however, the key role was to be played by a new institution not then known to Britain nor to any other part of continental North America. The plantation was not a transplanted English manor; it produced a specialized product to sell and not a variety of goods to be consumed locally. It established itself here before any other economic, political, administrative, educational, or religious institution became strong enough to flourish or even to survive. It was the mother factor in southern society, and this is why it is so important to understand its essential character and nature if we are to understand the system it built around itself.

V

Most Southerners have never physically lived within the bounds of a plantation estate, but I suggest that all properly designated as Southerners have lived within a "plantation system." There are and have been many other societies around the world in which the plantation isolate has been present, but in my reading of the literature I have not encountered any other society in which the expression "plantation system" has been so consistently and persistently used in both popular and academic circles as in the South. Hawaii has what might be called a system of plantations, but not, in the sense in which we understand the expression, a plantation system. In the South it is not an institution appearing on the periphery of another and older society as in Malaya and in the East Indies. On the contrary, it centered and formed whatever was distinctive about the South itself. In Brazil and elsewhere in Latin America the crown, the church, and the plantation seem to have competed for ultimate control of the social order.[8] In the South there was little else to contest its control. The king was far away and little concerned to claim and protect all his subjects. There was no powerful church with a traditionally recognized concern for souls.[9] About all that was left on this turbulent, disorderly southern frontier in the wilderness to interpose restraint in the relations between master and man was the ruth or aidôs of the master, those qualities of human nature which come into play when a man is almost totally free from any kind of institutional compulsion. Slaves were property, and a man can do what he will with his own unless inhibited by his own property interest or by some sentiment within himself.

But the lawless master and planter established law on his own plantation and increasingly engaged in various sorts of cooperation with neighboring despotisms as the frontier passed on and time brought common problems requiring common action. There was, for example, the problem of transporting and marketing the staple. Beyond the development of an economic order a moral order of mutual expectations and obligations, rights and duties, began to take form and to build themselves into a system of interrelated institutions the better to insure the institution's continuity and survival. The plantation system was in fact a plantation *survival* system intended to naturalize and legitimate the institution which stood at its center. Like the solar system with the sun at its center warming and holding its satellite planets in their several courses around it, the plantation came to center a system of attending and interacting institutions which it warmed and which in turn was warmed by them. The plantation system was not a series of disconnected institutions but an organism adapted to the situation in which people lived and carried on a common life. There were institutional forces of cohesion which bound them together and about which they later came to be conscious. They called this institutional complex the South.

In no kind of system, social or otherwise, can any single element be understood or be what it is apart from all the other elements or components of that system. The southern church and its religion was a part of the plantation system and so were other institutions such as the family, the school, the county and the state. Control of the system was exercised by consensus among a relatively small planter establishment.[10]

VI

The migration of Europeans and their settlement in that part of North America which became the South initially was predominantly masculine. As white women were imported and as the sexes evened out, white family life stabilized along income and class lines. Modeled after the European family it nevertheless underwent significant modifications as it adapted to frontier conditions. It underwent further modification as some men became *white* men vis-à-vis Indians and Negroes. It underwent further modification as some men became agricultural enterpreneurs, that is, planters, and masters not only of their white servants and black slaves but also of their families. The marked habit of command and skill in handling people was noted by visitors. From the beginning the planter families on their estates were highly isolated.[11] A planter in John Pendleton Kennedy's novel *Swallow Barn* voiced his opposition to a measure then before the legislature to improve the state's roads by declaring that "the home material of Virginia was never so good as when her roads were at their worst."

Ordinarily in the case of the small family farm the enterprise is bent toward the organization and requirements of the family, and this has been true in the South,[12] but in the case of the large estate the family ordinarily bends toward the organization and requirements of the enterprise. In Virginia the life of the planter family was geared to tobacco, in South Carolina and Mississippi to cotton; during the time of cultivation and harvesting wives and children took second place. But because there was no great amount of economic dependence upon other plantations producing the same staple in the same general area, such as has characterized neighboring small farms elsewhere, there was no extensive elaboration of local divisions of labor, and consequently there were few towns such as normally are required to integrate a variety of local economic activities.

But perhaps for this very reason white families, and particularly planter families, characteristically were united by the interweaving by marriage and other social ties into extensive kinship clans whose members often held membership in the same church. A range of between perhaps a half to a dozen differently surnamed families constituted a local community familism whose members were almost as much at home in the homes of each other as they were in their own homes. Incidentally, southern kinship has never been systematically investigated.

If the development of the plantation institution raised the dignity of many a commonplace European adventurer to a point approximating that of an English manorial lord and gave him an authority over his family and laborers greater than that of the lord, it had an opposite effect on the black male slave. This man was completely demoralized, incapable of asserting authority either as husband or father. Ultimate slavery is sexual slavery either when men are denied access to women except as managed studs or when women are forcibly used by men. Family life is incompatible with slavery and on the southern plantation the African family was pulverized.

A stable social order is stable because, for one important thing, its constituent families can be counted upon to conserve the old and the traditional. In the course of its development every new movement looking toward the institutionalization of new purposes and goals finds itself in opposition to the tradition-bearing family. The traditional family represents the *mores*, and the emerging institution is always more or less at war with them. In that process of "creative destruction" of which Joseph Schumpeter writes,[13] the family must be restructured to the point where it supports, rather than opposes, the organization and aims of the new institution. As a matter of fact, the "family" of the slave members of the prewar southern plantation might almost be said to have been the plantation itself somewhat

70

in the sense of the *familia rustica* in Roman society. The slave father was not the head and breadwinner; it was rather the planter who was looked to for material support as well as for discipline.[14] In the course of time what Frazier called the "natural" family organized around the Negro mother appeared.[15] Eventually the plantation obtained its new members by birth within rather than by recruitment from without. The plantation then came to form part of the habits and customs of the family to be transmitted to succeeding generations especially by the mother.

VII

All social life is, of course, education, but not every society provides that institutionalized form of communication and transmission which we call schools. The absence as well as the presence of formal education in schools in the social strata of a society tells something about the way such institutions function in the system. Those who labored in plantation fields were educated in the process of becoming what they were and had to be, but it was a bookless education without schools, the original and most effective expression of vocational guidance. There probably is a vocational aspect in the educational process of every society. In plantation society it has been a very prominent aspect. In early white indentured servitude, an outgrowth of English apprenticeship, there was a conscious vocational rationalization later expressed in the claim that the plantation itself was the proper school for servants and slaves. Provision for the more formal education in schools for this class was not a matter to be entertained; but if entertained at all, to be opposed as useless or even dangerous. When developments came to force the establishment of schools the principle accepted was that of education for greater efficiency in agricultural or mechanical labor.

Perhaps men generally are more largely educated by what they have to do to make a living than they are by their schools; in stable, isolated societies there is relatively little need for formal education. But when the society is becoming part of a larger world where there is change and movement, more formal education becomes necessary. For those whose business it was to plan and market the crop it was necessary to keep up with the market and to this end some amount of literacy was essential, but this was not necessarily obtained through formal schooling.[16] Before the War Between the States the percentage of literacy among slaveholders appeared much greater than among non-slaveholders.[17] A degree of literacy and education gained through informal as well as formal channels in order to make needed adjustments and decisions characterized Negro as well as white operators and landowners. This has continued to be the case.[18]

Well-to-do planters along the seaboard might employ tutors at home and then send their sons to European universities to acquire a certain amount of classical intellectual fodder beyond the practical requirements of plantation administration, but lesser members of this class in the interior patronized academies and agitated for state universities nearer them. The prestige colleges and universities of New England were private institutions, but in the South they became state universities established by planter members of the legislatures for their sons. Thus "college life became an important feature of the Old South," wrote H. C. Nixon, "especially of plantation society. . . . The slavocracy was more interested in higher education for the few than in effective secondary education for the many. . . . From the same background most of the colleges of the South have received a strong religious heritage, chiefly Protestant, and a respect for the form and organization of religion, though not necessarily for independent religious thought." [19] The church affiliated colleges of the South were much more democratically oriented than the state universities but they too operated under the shadow of the plantation. The need for military academies and colleges to support a racial hierarchy with its large strata of unfree agricultural workers at its base should be apparent.

VIII

Many of the patriotic county historians of the South described the county of which they wrote as one of "great plantations." Of course, there are counties in which plantations were or are not physically present and which were characterized by their relative independency, such as "the independent republic of Horry" County in South Carolina and "the free state of Jones" County in Mississippi which, tradition says, seceded from Mississippi during the War Between the States. But the county as a primary social as well as governmental unit in the South undoubtedly developed as part of the plantation system. Local administrative units originally called baronies in Maryland and elsewhere, parishes in Louisiana and occasionally in Florida, hundreds, shires, or cities in Virginia, eventually settled for the form if not the name of county. River and road transportational development in relation to land acquisition and the marketing of the staple in the tidewater South was the basis of the organization of the county.[20] There might be something in the nature of formal subdivisions of the county such as the "beat" in Mississippi, but in fact the county began as a sort of local organization of plantations which were the actual subdivisions. The township as a functional unit was a Reconstruction imposition.

The county, over much of the southern territory, became a creature of tradition and stained itself indelibly upon the form of society.[21] Often it was ruled by a coterie of county families whose members left office only to be replaced by other members of the clan.[22] They praised themselves for their unselfish devotion to public service. In the later plantation South, Indian enemies were supplanted by an inner enemy, the unfree laborers of the estates against whom defense was even more imperative. That social type, more or less peculiar to the system, the county sheriff, continues his traditional role to this day as recent events testify. Early county sheriffs as well as other officers of the law often found it convenient to serve writs and warrants on Sundays when it was easier to find delinquents attending parish churches. Following the model of the ideal planter the sheriff and his deputies often rode horseback to symbolize their connection with the aristocracy. In 1711 Lancaster County, Virginia, ordered that freedmen and laborers be prevented from keeping horses and breeding mares and limited their ownership to persons who owned or rented a certain amount of property.[23] The sheriff could and did use "landlord" law and the organization of the plantation after as well as before the War Between the States to make arrests (occasionally the planter or overseer did this for him) but he might well be careful not to make arrests during the cotton-picking season. He was likely to be well paid for his services, especially in the Black Belt counties. In "Imperial Bolivar" County, Mississippi, in the 1930s he had a net income of forty thousand dollars, ten times the salary of the governor of the state.[24]

That same establishment which the sheriff served could be confident that the courts could be relied upon to maintain its authority and protect its interests in both legal and extralegal ways.[25] Planter control of state government was not always so complete as was their control over county government in predominantly plantation areas, but it was strong enough to effect the secession of eleven states by the middle of the last century. And it is not without significance that of the first twelve presidents of the United States eight were members of the planter class.

74

IX

In a developing social system where intermarriage within class and race limitations linked families at various points with other institutions in the larger society, giving the plantation points of reference with these other institutions, it was inevitable and even necessary that the church and whatever brand of doctrine it offered should find a place and a function. From diverse backgrounds and later organizational differentiations, Protestants and Catholics, as well as Jews articulated into the system and served it. The Protestant denominations were sharply competitive with each other, white denominations with each other and Negro denominations with each other, and all with the Catholic "enemy." Almost every minister and priest was a religious politician. They fought minor battles with each other, but planters, lesser farmers, poor whites, factors, ministers, priests, and laymen united in an acceptance of the legitimacy of the system and of the values it embodied. Even the old-time Negro preacher was an integral and useful part of the system, especially in the postwar period. Generally all supported it in the only way they could support it, if their churches hoped to survive, by seeking to transfer attention from the ills of this world to salvation in the next, by blessing the pious allegiance of ordinary people, by defining the "good man" whose superior achievement in reconciling religion and common practice singled him out for special praise, by urging obedience to the caesars of the day and patience in the face of poverty, trial, and tribulation. A faith was harnessed to canonize the system and to brand as atheistic any threat of change in it. That faith was inevitable and deterministic; denominational membership was, of course, optional. All church members were at the same time members of the community and as such were unable to compartmentalize their religious beliefs and practices from the interests and attitudes they held as members of other institutions.

Something special should be said about the Negro church and its religion in the system, but I have not found in the literature any significantly insightful or satisfying treatment of the subject although much has been written about it. So far as I know no fundamental point of view has informed this literature. But I suggest that if there is a line to be drawn, however lightly, between the ethos of various groups in the plantation South with regard to religious experience and orientation it will not be drawn between Protestant denominations or even between Protestant and Catholic but between white and black. The change-oriented black Protestantism and the continuity-oriented white Protestantism and Catholicism defined each other within the *same* system; the system supplied a basis for the kind of variation from it taken by its black segment. One has to look for this kind of variation not in the form or creed of Negro churches, but in its mood and spirit, in its philosophy of life generally. This is a difficult thing to get at and to state. I expect it has been there since the black man came in chains to these shores, but it is especially prominent today in black militancy.

Students of the black man in Africa have called attention to the role of the Christian missions there as an institution around which detribalized and lost natives often reestablished themselves into something like another tribe of Christian brothers and sisters. The missionaries had relatively little success among tightly organized tribal blacks. In America, where all imported blacks were, in the nature of the case, detribalized and disorganized, it is not surprising that the church, an "invisible institution" within the visibly white controlled and plantation connected church,[26] became for them the center of reorganization. It was in this institution that Negro slaves from diverse African tribal backgrounds began to find some meaning for their existence, and it was this institution that enlisted their deepest loyalties. Here a man might find and maintain a conception of himself as one of dignity and one which gave him a sense of individual worth.

Only four years after the coming of the first Negroes in 1619 there were black church members in the Jamestown settlement in Virginia,[27] but the separate "invisible church" took shape in the praise-house and the shout on individual seaboard plantations. Conversion to the religious forms of the white man spread under the influence of Baptist and Methodist preachers who presented Christianity to the blacks in a simple, emotional appeal which, combined with their own special life experience, developed into religious theater and came to characterize the folk-culture of Negroes generally. One interesting and important product of this culture was the spiritual and another was the folk-sermon which, so far as I know, was unique to the Negro Protestant South. James Weldon Johnson attempted to reproduce several of these sermons in verse.[28] Many of them, such as "The Valley of Dry Bones," were repeated and passed along like the spirituals with modifications from one community to another. They were not created *for* the people by the preacher; they were created *by* the people and belonged to the congregation to be delivered by the preacher on demand or by special invitation.

But perhaps precisely because of the appearance of the spiritual, the folk-sermon, the strong emphasis upon heaven rather than hell, and other manifestations of quaint differences from the usual white religious expression, the Negro church and its religion has been suspect by whites almost from the beginning. Christianity is the religion of the white man who has been embarrassed by its injunction to go out and preach the Gospel to the heathen of all the world. But were the heathen human and rational enough to accept it? The question arose in connection with the American Indian and the African Negro and has never really been satisfactorily settled. How can we whites, the guardians of pure Christianity, be sure that the conversion is genuine? We may not resort to the Inquisition as did the Spaniards with respect to the Jews and the Moors, but we have our doubts and freely express them in joke and ridicule.[29] Or we may champion the excellence of Negro Christianity with somewhat more fervor than is justified.

Attention is focused upon the differences between white and black religious behavior in both Protestantism and Catholicism when the truly significant thing is, perhaps, the remarkable extent to which the religion of the Negro in America has recapitulated the Christian cycle as it has turned many times before and continues, in the storefront churches of the cities, for example, to start all over again. For Christianity is *par excellence* the religion of the outcast and the defeated. In Rome it was taken up by the slaves, the slum-dwellers, and the poor who were especially blessed. The religion of the Negro in America developed under much the same conditions as primitive Christianity itself.[30] It came to segregate itself into an independent church among the free Negroes of northern cities before the War Between the States. After emancipation independent churches in the South absorbed the "invisible church" of plantation society and became the chief repositories of the traditions and aspirations of the black masses.

I think it is well-nigh impossible really to understand the development of the Negro church and its religion in the South as a counter to the white church and its religion without reference to the plantation and its system both before and after emancipation. The imagery and realities of the plantation lived on; God figured as a Great Planter in much the same way, perhaps, as he figured as a Great Lord in Britain from the time of the Roman missionaries onward. Allison Davis noted that "the analogy between the white landlord and the partriarchal Old Testament God was frequently used by rural ministers. . . . Following a prayer an officer in one church said that when each man came up for his reward in the after-life, he would receive just what he merited, adding, 'Ef you worked hard, you know you due yo' pay, but if you ain't, you know dere ain't no reward for you. Ain't no use goin' tuh de office unless you done made yo' crop.' " [31]

X

By 1830 the southern states had become, as John C. Calhoun noted, "an aggregate . . . of communities, not of individuals. Every plantation is a little community, . . . These small communities aggregated make the State in all." [32] Each plantation had its own notions of what was right and wrong; its own conception of the proper roles of its different characters; its own "little tradition," each varying a little from that of every other. A certain standardizing process was initiated when the student sons of planters gathered together, talked, and debated at the state colleges and universities, but probably much more important was the development of orthogenetic plantation capital cities[33] such as Williamsburg, Charleston, Savannah, Mobile, and New Orleans. Planters and people from the provinces generally went back and forth between these sacred cities and their local neighborhoods as in other great religious cultures men made periodic pilgrimages to Mecca, Lhasa, Rome, or some other holy city. In these cities the little traditions of individual plantations were reshaped and articulated by poets, novelists, theologians, ministers, scholars, and editors into a "great tradition" which came to be generally accepted all over the South and which gave Southerners their stock clichés, platitudes, and rationalizations. The tobacco, cotton, and sugar factors in these cities also made planters and farmers more aware of their common economic interests. The individual plantations fed their experiences, beliefs, problems, and lore to the wise men and the prophets of the capitals; these experiences and this lore came back in standardized form as ideology and conviction. The plantation system was achieving a culture for the South which was to differentiate it from other regions of the United States and perhaps of the world. While a social system is not always bound to a particular territory or geographical space, the fact that the plantation system was spatially defined did have a decisive influence upon its formation and maintenance. The plantation system and the South became almost synonymous expressions, the land of God corresponding to the land of his true worshipers.

A common culture arose in and from this system, but social scientists have defined culture in many different ways. Here it may be suggested that a culture is a system of conventional understandings general enough to influence everyone included within it. The number of people included within it may be small or large; the major cultures of the world include large numbers of people but with subcultural deviations. Millions of people have grown up within the culture or subculture of the South and have known no other, or very little of any other. Here an expression of the Christian religion has, perhaps more than any other force, operated to transform a heterogeneous aggregate into a homogeneous society binding together its segments and separate institutions and to build and preserve the morale of the people.[34] It has helped the system take over the children of all classes, keep them in their proper stations, enforce conformity to old custom, and preserve the order of power relations.

At the level of culture, life carries conviction and the deep assumption shared with all others in the community that the world will go on substantially in the same manner as it has so far, that what is accepted as valid up to now will continue to be valid. In the light of today's rapid change and uncertainty to read diaries and other documents written in the old Plantation South is almost to have one's breath taken away by the sense of certainty, the assurance that the then order of things would continue until the Day of Judgment. But this structure of shared assumptions tends to get lost in written rendition or even in verbalization. There was no doubt. All others will agree with us and with all that is personal to us and at our own valuation. One speaks with no reservations. To all orthodox statements there could be but one reply, "of course." In a culture so conceived the speech of the naïve one itself becomes behavior, in the elementary sense of that term, rather than explanation.

The culture of a society such as that of the Old South continuing into the New is to be found in the truths which are held to be self-evident, truths that hardly need to be examined and explained, truths held by a people innocent of their own character but sure of themselves. A poet might write of the ordinary people of the South, old and new, very much as Monk Gibbon wrote of French peasants:

> Those going home at dusk
>   Along the lane,
> After the day's warm work,
>   Do not complain.
>
> Were you to say to them,
>   "What does it mean?
> What is it all about,
>   This troubled dream?"
>
> They would not understand,
>   They'd go their way,
> Or, if they spoke at all,
>   They'd surely say:
>
> "Dawn is the time to rise,
>   Days are to earn
> Bread and the midday rest,
>   Dusk to return;
>
> "To be content, to pray,
>   To hear songs sung
> Or to make wayside love,
>   If one is young.

"All from the good God comes,
   All then is good;
Sorrow is known to Him,
   And understood."

One who has questioned all,
   And was not wise,
Might be ashamed to meet
   Their quiet eyes.

All is so clear to them.
   All is so plain;
Those who go home at dusk,
   Along the lane.[35]

If naïveté be the subjective aspect of culture then we have in the endless number of stories and items which have appeared in newspapers, pamphlets, journals, and books for over two hundred years a vast literature exhibiting southern religiosity. The quickest way to get a few of these items would be to consult the Americana sections in each issue of *The American Mercury* during the days when editor H. L. Mencken was printing them in order to ridicule *Boobus Americanus* as he called us. It is not necessary to share his purpose to appreciate the cultural significance of this material. Here are a few of the items:

From Mississippi it was reported that "the Rev. William McCarty, now 96 years old, was called upon two weeks ago to preach at the funeral of a notorious sinner, a relative of Mrs. Levy Laird. The Reverend Mr. McCarty preached frankly on the sins of the deceased man and, instead of assuring the mourners that he was going to Heaven, boldly stated that he would go to a much hotter place. He exhorted the younger people to live righteously lest they go there too. The stuff that the Reverend Mr. McCarty was putting on her dead relative grew too hot for Mrs. Laird. She reached out and snatched at the preacher. When he ducked, she pursued him, and finally was successful in tearing most of his clothes, smashing his hat, and scratching him up so viciously that he had to see a physician. He had Mrs. Laird arrested. She was fined and sentenced to a term in the workhouse for disturbing public worship." [36]

The naïve person assumes that what he is naïve about, that is, what he takes for granted, is taken for granted by everyone else who is normal and sane. Thus from Tennessee: "A lot of bright-colored bathing suits, decks of cards and novels were missing from Madisonville homes today. They were burned in front of the Baptist church yesterday following a baptismal service in which thirty-five were baptised. The Reverend W. A. Carroll, who conducted a three-week revival, asked those in attendance to bring their bathing suits, cards and cheap novels. While 'I'll Never Turn Back' was being sung the Reverend Carroll set fire to them." [37]

It is not what United States Senator Cameron Morrison of North Carolina expressly says that is significant in the following but what, as one reads between the lines, he regards as obviously just about what any North Carolinian would expect of a man in public office: "I got to be Governor and lived in the executive mansion for four years, and while I was there God gave me a good, noble woman for my wife. She has some money. She, too, had seen much service and as a nurse had ministered to suffering humanity. We have retired to our farm and there she fights the devil through the Presbyterian church, and whatever money is left and I get hold of I use to fight the devil through the Democratic party. And I tell her they're about the same anyway." [38]

From Danville, Virginia, it was reported that "the Rev. McKendrie Long, who is conducting revivals here, warned tobacco chewers about their chances of salvation. They may all go to Heaven, he said, but 'they will have to go to Hell to expectorate, as the Lord does not allow spitting on the streets of gold.' " [39]

It is not so much what people say but what they are taking for granted when they say what they say that exhibits the culture of the society in which they live. The sensitive observer, especially one who ventures into the South from outside, today senses something different, maybe something special, something pervasive, something old and tenacious in the *pietas* of southern society. It is the Old South continuing on into the New.

XI

I have sought to probe the historical and cultural roots of the southern church and its religion the better to understand some of my own experiences and of many others like me. It appears that southern society, like societies generally, is of a piece, an entanglement of institutions of which the church was and is one of the most important. Along with the family, the school or college, and governmental units it was a satellite of the plantation institution and functioned effectively within the plantation system. The institution which centered the system utilized unfree or semifree labor and, to the extent it continues to linger on, its labor practices still are suspect. As an economic institution it depended upon a national and even international market for its staples, a market which underwent and continues to undergo change from time to time as supply, demand, competition, substitutes, fashion, and machine methods change or are introduced. Today we are seeing the plantation disappear or erode as cities grow and southern people, black and white, move into them, as sharecropping and tenancy are eliminated as slavery was before them, and as mechanization proceeds apace. Originally an institution of the frontier, the plantation was bound to change and at last disappear as the frontier moved on and new forces gathered in its wake. That it continued to function as the center of a system in one form or another for over two hundred years, surviving even a devastating civil war, is the remarkable fact, but even over this period of time it has not been a completely stable and unvarying center. It is as though in the solar system the sun dimmed or blacked out leaving its planet satellites to move out of their age-old orbits. The plantation no longer centers a system of satellite institutions; since the turn of the century and especially since World War I, each institution is moving out of old orbits into new directions. Kinship and family life, probably the most stable element in every social structure, are undergoing modification as land changes hands and migration turns cityward. The race of plantation laborers, formerly subordinated, is now winning its civil rights, and institutions, especially schools, are being racially integrated. The school is no longer "our school"; it belongs to the impersonal state. In an age of rapid transportation and communication local town and county governmental units find themselves in trouble, administratively and financially; planters have lost or are losing control to "courthouse gangs" and to poorer white and black voters and officeholders. The bell in the country church steeple may still be there; but all too often it no longer summons the families of the neighborhood to worship; the church may remain as merely a site for the annual homecoming of the widely scattered family and clan members. We may expect Protestant and Catholic church tribalism, white and black, to continue to offer congregational fellowship along social class and economic level of living lines and continue the struggle to conserve whatever principles of certainty the fathers found good. Even here, however, change is evident as new sects arise, as new class lines form, and as the urban church turns away from the doctrines and practices of its rural heritage. The southern church is at least altering its direction as the forces and vital needs that put it in the system in the first place are no longer functional.

85

One thinks of the prophetic line of W. B. Yeats, "Things fall apart; the centre cannot hold." Of course, the social as well as the geographical South is still here and will be here for a long time to come; there is always continuity as well as change. But, like a fortified city, its walls are down and its institutions stand exposed to criticism, rational and otherwise. Southern geocentrism will not want to admit it, but the plantation as the center of a social system developed no great civilization. It was a moral and intellectual failure. In time the South will get another system perhaps this time centered around its evolving constellation of cities and possibly just as full of piety and illusion as the old one, but which may bring its institutions into some greater degree of cohesion again. Some will call the movement toward a new and different system progress and be led to speak of another and newer New South promising a higher civilization while others will look back nostalgically to a lost Golden Age. The various expressions of the southern church and its religion will debate the problems presented by continuity versus change because it will be called upon to sustain and help integrate whatever system of society may be in store for us. It continues to be important to experience, to observe, to read the books and the daily newspapers, and to try to understand.

NOTES

1. Kenneth Burke, *Permanence and Change: An Anatomy of Purpose* (Indianapolis: Bobbs-Merrill, 1965), p. 74.

2. The opinion of the Reverend H. C. Morrison of Asbury College is representative. He doubted whether there was "another territory of like area beneath the sun, where there is a stronger, better faith in the Bible, where the Sabbath is better observed, where a larger per cent. of the people attend church, where virtue in womanhood and honesty in

manhood are more common and command a better premium" than in the South. Kenneth K. Bailey, *Southern White Protestantism in the Twentieth Century* (New York: Harper, 1964), p. 24.

3. Robert K. Merton, "The Unanticipated Consequences of Purposeful Social Action," *American Sociological Review* I (December, 1936), 894-904; William Graham Sumner, "Religion and the Mores," in *War and Other Essays* (New Haven: Yale University Press, 1919), chap. 5.

4. Bailey, *Southern White*, p. 24.

5. As late as 1935 Edwin McNeill Poteat, Jr., could write: "In spite of considerable ecclesiastical differences the theology of the South is the same in its broad essentials among all the religious groups. Whether one meets in a Quaker Meeting House in Guilford County, North Carolina, or in a Methodist Church in Savannah, or in St. Louis Cathedral in New Orleans, the basal religious philosophy is the same. Scratch any sectarian skin and the same orthodox blood flows. This is what accounts in a measure for the uniform dullness of most of the sectarian papers." In W. T. Couch, ed., *Culture in the South* (Chapel Hill: University of North Carolina Press, 1935), p. 261.

6. Seymour Martin Lipset, *Political Man: The Social Basis of Politics* (Garden City: Doubleday Anchor Books, 1960), pp. 273-74.

7. Everett Hughes, *The Chicago Real Estate Board: The Growth of an Institution* (Chicago: University of Chicago Press, 1931), Preface.

8. Stanley M. Elkins, *Slavery: A Problem in American Institutional Life* (Chicago: University of Chicago Press, 1959), p. 81. But cf. T. Lynn Smith, *Brazil: People and Institutions* (Baton Rouge: Louisiana State University Press, 1954), *passim*.

9. Elkins, *Slavery*, 201-2; Winthrop D. Jordan speaks of the Anglican church in early Virginia as "an organizational mon-

strosity. . . . The Anglican Church was 'established' in the southern colonies, though the establishment was particularly shaky in North Carolina and Georgia. In Virginia the Church's position was relatively firm, but even there it could scarcely be termed a powerful institution; . . . the vestrymen were normally the leading planters of the parish. The established Anglican Church of Virginia . . . was in large measure dominated by slaveholders." *White Over Black* (Chapel Hill: University of North Carolina Press, 1968), pp. 206-7.

10. Wesley F. Craven, *Southern Colonies in the 17th Century, 1607-1689* (Baton Rouge: Louisiana State University Press, 1949), pp. 153, 159, 170-72, 274-78; Philip A. Bruce, *Institutional History of Virginia in the Seventeenth Century,* Vol. I (New York: Putnam, 1910), p. 468; George M. Brydon, *Virginia's Mother Church and the Political Conditions Under Which It Grew,* Vol. I (Richmond: Virginia Historical Society, 1947), pp. 94, 96, 232; Frank Lawrence Owsley, *Plain Folk of the Old South* (Baton Rouge: Louisiana State University Press, 1949), chap. 1; James McBride Dabbs, *Who Speaks for the South?* (New York: Funk and Wagnalls, 1964), chap. 8.

11. Somers, speaking of Mississippi, said, "The farms and plantations, of which there are many, seem to have been picked out, far apart from one another, in the recesses of the woods, without making any great impression on the natural wilderness of the country." Robert Somers, *The Southern States Since the War, 1870-1871* (New York: Macmillan, 1871), p. 240.

12. Owsley, *Plain Folk,* pp. 136-37.

13. Joseph Schumpeter, *Capitalism, Socialism, and Democracy* (New York: Harper, 1942), chap. 7.

14. See Edgar T. Thompson, "The Natural History of Agricultural Labor in the South," in *American Studies in Honor of W. K. Boyd,* D. K. Jackson, ed. (Durham, N. C.: Duke University Press, 1940), pp. 156-57.

15. E. Franklin Frazier, *The Negro Family in the United States* (Chicago: The University of Chicago Press, 1939), chaps. 2, 3.

16. See Edgar T. Thompson, "Comparative Education in Colonial Areas, with Special Reference to Plantation and Mission Frontiers," in *Education and the Cultural Process*, Charles S. Johnson, ed., reprinted from *The American Journal of Sociology*, XLVIII (May, 1943), 82-93.

17. See Blanche Henry Clark, *The Tennessee Yeoman, 1840-1860* (Nashville: Vanderbilt University Press, 1942), p. 16.

18. "There is a much greater tendency for Negroes to be able to read and write when they independently operate small farms, or if a family or so of them work for a single white family, than there is if they are grouped together in large numbers as wage hands, croppers, or share tenants on the plantations." T. Lynn Smith, *The Population of Louisiana*, Louisiana Bulletin no. 293 (Baton Rouge: Louisiana State University, 1937).

19. H. C. Nixon, "Colleges and Universities," in *Culture in the South*, W. T. Couch, ed. (Chapel Hill: University of North Carolina Press, 1935), p. 229.

20. Lewis W. Wilhem, "Local Institutions of Maryland," *Johns Hopkins University Studies in History and Political Science, 1885*, Vol. III, p. 65; Edward Ingle, "Local Institutions of Virginia," *ibid.*, pp. 45-46.

21. "Prior to 1851 the government of Maryland was in theory and practice a loose confederation of counties and cities similar in spirit to the national government under the Articles of Confederation." Chester Maxey, "The Political Integration of Metropolitan Communities," *National Municipal Review* XI (1922), 230. Several of the counties of this State are peninsulas which jut down into the Chesapeake Bay; the strong county solidarity of the State probably has this insular influence as its origin. Maryland virtually ratified the Federal constitution by counties. John V. L. McMahon, *An Historical View of the Government of Maryland* (Baltimore: 1831), p. 464.

22. "From 1670 to 1691 every official position in Henrico county [in Virginia] was filled by a member of the Randolph family or two other families. Four families got most of the military offices of the county. Similar conditions prevailed in all the older countries where certain families had been long enough to establish powerful and political connections." Arthur W. Calhoun, *A Social History of the American Family*, Vol. I (Cleveland: The Arthur H. Clark Co., 1917), p. 233.

23. Francis Joseph Tschan, "The Virginia Planter, 1700-1775." Ph.D. dissertation, University of Chicago, 1916, pp. 334-35: If the horse was the Cadillac of the plantation gentry, as has been said, he was also the Model T Ford of the Methodist circuit rider in the back country.

24. Arthur F. Raper, *The Tragedy of Lynching* (Chapel Hill: University of North Carolina Press, 1933), p. 104.

25. Joseph Rosenstein, "Government and Social Structure in a Deep South Community," Master's thesis, University of Chicago, 1941, p. 23; Charles S. Sydnor, *Gentlemen Freeholders: Political Practices in Washington's Virginia* (Chapel Hill: University of North Carolina Press, 1952), *passim*.

26. E. Franklin Frazier, *The Negro Church in America* (New York: Schocken Books, 1963), chap. 1.

27. E. B. Reuter, *The American Race Problems: A Study of the Negro*, rev. ed. (New York: Thomas Y. Crowell Company, 1938), p. 313.

28. *God's Trombones: Seven Negro Sermons in Verse* (New York: The Viking Press, 1927).

29. It is perhaps not unlike the separation of "European" and "non-European" Catholicism in Brazil. Cf. Donald Warren, Jr., "The Negro and Religion in Brazil," *Race*, VI (January, 1965), 99 ff.

30. Unlike their white masters who continued a core of fixed Christian tradition inherited from Europe, the black man in America took on a new creed, a new God, and especially

a new Savior with the kind of fervor and seriousness that characterized the early Christians. See *God Struck Me Dead*, Social Science Source Documents, no. 2, Social Science Institute (Nashville: Fisk University, 1945). The note of militancy which perhaps has been present in American Negro Christianity since colonial days has recently been greatly accentuated. See Joseph R. Washington, Jr., *Black Religion* (Boston: Beacon Press, 1964); and James H. Cone, *Black Theology and Black Power* (New York: Seabury Press, 1969); Hart M. Nelsen, *et al.* eds., *The Black Church in America* (New York: Basic Books, 1971).

31. Allison Davis, "The Relation Between Color Caste and Economic Stratification in Two 'Black' Plantation Counties," Ph.D. dissertation, University of Chicago, 1942, p. 42.

32. Richard K. Crallé, ed., *The Works of John C. Calhoun*, Vol. III (New York: D. Appleton, 1851-1870), p. 180.

33. I am indebted to Robert Redfield and Milton B. Singer for the distinctions between the "little tradition" and the "great tradition" and between orthogenetic cities and heterogenetic cities. "The Cultural Role of Cities," *Economic Development and Cultural Change*, III (October, 1954), 53-73.

34. Paul Tillich argues that culture is the sort of order existing in a society which has a cult or a religion. It is the form or shape that religion takes. *Theology of Culture* (New York: Oxford University Press, 1968), chap. 4; *Systematic Theology*, Vol. III (Chicago: University of Chicago Press, 1963), p. 95.

35. Monk Gibbon, *For Daws to Peck At* (New York: Dodd, Mead and Co., n.d.), p. 41. By permission of Victor Gollancz, Ltd., London.

36. *American Mercury* XXVIII (January, 1933), 35.

37. *Ibid.*, XXVII (October, 1932), 163.

38. *Ibid.*, XXVI (May, 1932), 52.

39. *Ibid.*, XXVI (July, 1932), 313.

4
WOMEN, RELIGION AND SOCIAL CHANGE IN THE SOUTH 1830-1930

The significance of evangelical Protestantism in southern history and culture has long been a subject of interest. The history of southern women, just now beginning to be studied, may throw new light on this old topic. The personal documents of literate southern women contribute a new angle of vision from which to view the question of the role religion played in the society and in the culture, and in the vast social changes which occurred in the years after 1830.

In antebellum times such women were intensely preoccupied with personal piety, with the need for salvation and for godly behavior. Men of the time had similar concerns, but except for ministers of the church a man's daily behavior was not expected to reflect so fully the depth of his religious commitment. The image of the ideal Christian woman was very close to the image of the ideal southern lady so that religion strongly reinforced the patriarchal culture.

The primary social concern of antebellum southern women, stemming in part from their Christian commitment, was with African slavery. Placed, as plantation wives were, in close juxtaposition to slaves, responsible for their physical and spiritual well-being, many southern women became secret abolitionists. When the Civil War came it was not uncommon for women to view it as God's punishment of the South for the sin of owning slaves. Women often described emancipation as the will of God.

For the rest of the nineteenth century and well into the twentieth religion continued to be a central aspect of many women's lives, but its form gradually changed from intense personal piety to a concern for the salvation of the heathen and for social problems. In their missionary societies and in the Woman's Christian Temperance Union many southern women came bit by bit to develop something which was in practice, if not in theology, a social gospel. In making this transition they also remade themselves. By experimenting with new kinds of behavior they developed new strength of personality and capacity for leadership hitherto not much encouraged by the society. The process is interesting, and throws considerable light on the interaction between religion and women's emancipation.

Everywhere in the Anglo-American culture of 1830 "woman's sphere" was sharply defined and very restricted. Nowhere was this more evident than in the American South. When Sidney Mead, a historian of religion, asserts that one of the universal images of the period was that of the "free individual . . . the person with full opportunity to develop his every latent possibility or natural power," it would appear that he is simply asserting that American history is the history only of American men.[1] Certainly no such universal image prevailed with respect to the female half of the population.

Far from being encouraged to develop her latent possibilities, it was the prevailing view that woman existed for

the benefit of her family and that her life should be conducted in complete submissiveness to the will of her husband. Neither the culture nor the law viewed her as a free
individual, nor did many women themselves glimpse such a
possibility.

Thomas Nelson Page supposed himself to be writing not
fiction, but social history, when he described an antebellum
Virginia matron:

Her life was one long act of devotion,—devotion to God,
devotion to her husband, devotion to her children, devotion
to her servants, to the poor, to humanity. Nothing happened
within the range of her knowledge that her sympathy did not
reach and her charity and wisdom did not ameliorate. She was
the head and foot of the church. . . . The training of her
children was her work. She watched over them, inspired them,
led them, governed them; her will impelled them; her word
to them, as to her servants was law. She reaped the reward
. . . their sympathy and tenderness were hers always, and they
worshipped her.[2]

The southern women who left a record, the women who
wrote letters and diaries, stories and poems, to whom sermons were addressed and eulogies written were expected
to be meek, mild, quiet outside their homes, self-abnegating, kind to all, and to accept their husbands as lord and
master.

The imagery is plain. Precisely the virtues which were
attributed to the perfect woman were those demanded of
the perfect Christian. The church effectively reinforced the
cultural image of woman. Christian perfection was seen as
obedience to the will of God—and women were frequently
reminded of the necessity for inhabiting the "sphere to
which God had appointed them." "All sin consists in selfish-
ness and all holiness or virtue in disinterested benevolence"
seems to have been the operative theology of many antebellum southern women.

The demands for Christian perfection were transmitted largely through the evangelical churches. Baptists and Methodists together claimed over a million members in the South in 1855, so that with some help from Presbyterians they clearly dominated the religious life of the section. The mechanisms were familiar ones: Sunday church, midweek prayer meetings, revivals, and periodic love-feasts. That these gatherings served many functions in addition to religious ones we take for granted: In a thinly populated society everything from horse trading to courtship was conducted at church, as well as simple sociability, gossip, and politics. In addition to all these things however, women communicants seem to have absorbed a common theological outlook. This point of view was reinforced by the religious periodicals, including some written expressly for women. The themes which recur in the diaries and letters of antebellum southern women are familiar to any student of evangelical religion: the emphasis upon prayer, contemplation, and Bible reading; the need for constant cultivation of submissiveness to the will of an all-powerful God; the need for subduing the self and practicing goodness to others; the importance of raising children to fear God; the achievement of conversion and secure salvation; and a strong sense of one's own innate wickedness. For salvation both faith and works seem to have been required. Whether they were aware of the label or not most southern women were Arminians who believed in man's participation in his own salvation. Add to this a firm belief in life after death, and the constellation of generally accepted beliefs is complete.

A mosaic constructed from letters and diaries is revealing. "I feel this day heavy and sad and I would ask myself why and the answer is I feel cold in religious matters oh why am I thus?" [3] "I feel that I am worthless and through the merits of Christ's all-atoning blood alone can I be saved." [4] "Mr. B. [her husband] says we must try to live holier. Oh that I could. Spent some time today reading, weeping and praying. . . ." [5] "Help me O Lord for I am poor and weak, help me for I am desolate, in Thee alone have I hope." [6] "As for myself I find my heart so full of sinful feelings that I am ready to say 'I am chief of sinners'. . . ." [7] "Lord I feel that my heart is a cage of unclean beasts." [8]

In a time when infants and children died very easily, women found comfort in the assurance that God had some purpose in these deaths. "As you say we have been greatly afflicted," wrote a mother whose two children had died, "we dare not ask *why* but strive to say to our crushed hearts 'Be still and know that I am God. . . .' I trust our Gracious God will preserve me from the slightest rebellion against his holy will—will you pray for me? . . ." [9] "I see so much of sin, so many things to correct, that I almost despair of being a perfect christian. . . ." [10] "Oh! for an increased degree of peace to know and do my redeemers will, to live more as I should. . . ." [11] The biblical verse most frequently quoted in southern women's diaries was from Jeremiah: "The heart is deceitful above all things and desperately wicked: who can know it?" [12] There are references to sins too awful even to be recorded in a private journal, accompanied by allusions to cold hearts.

Many women assumed that if they were not happy and contented in the "sphere to which God had appointed them" it must be their own fault and that by renewed effort they could do better. "My besetting sins are a roving mind and an impetuous spirit," wrote one woman whose diary is filled with admonitions to herself to be systematic, diligent, prudent, economical, and patient with her servants.[13] In another context she might have been proud of her imaginative reach and her spontaneity.

Josephine Clay Habersham, a gentle and gifted woman who presided with skill and dignity over a large plantation in eastern Georgia and whose fitness for the role society offered her might be measured by her spontaneous notation:

"I wish always to have a sweet babe on my lap," still felt it necessary to cultivate constantly a cheerful spirit and to ask God for help with her "dull and wayward heart." [14]

The Summer is over! Have I improved it as I should have done? Have I improved my children? Let me put these questions to myself in the privacy of my room and ask God's forgiveness that I am not a *more faithful* servant.[15]

A young girl was already well on the way to the typical woman's view of life:

Oh, we young ladies are all so surface like, so useless; I pray God I may be useful, only useful, I feel that I can say with Evangeline often, 'I have no wish nor desire but to follow meekly with reverent steps the footprints of my Redeemer,' and yet how I fail oh so sadly, many are the vain desires that every now and then trouble this prevailing one, and my flesh is so weak, I am always failing. . . .[16]

Women whose families and friends would have credited them with a "spotless life," were themselves convinced that their souls harbored serpents.

Oh that I might be delivered from the serpent's power— that God . . . would put enmity between me & the serpent— his folds are around my limbs; his sting in my heart. Today has not been without profit. I have reviewed my besetting sins —repented—and resolved this week at least to make battle against them. How proud & happy I could feel at the close of it, to find that in God's strength I have opposed my foes successfully.[17]

My way of late has been hedged up and my mind has seemed sunken with a state of apathy from which I can with difficulty arouse myself. I feel sure that my present state is owing to my own neglect of duty and fearful transgression of God's Holy law. And although the desire of my heart is to love and to serve him yet I am conscious of the world and its cares have too large a share of my time and affections. . . .[18]

Sudden death was not confined to children and the necessity for being ready to die at any moment was deeply felt. For religious women this meant one had to be "saved." The concern was not only for themselves but for all the members of the family, especially those who had not yet felt the experience of religious conversion.

After church I partook of the Lord's supper and benefited to an unusual degree. Oh! for an increased degree of peace to know and do as my redeemer wills, to live more as I should. More to the glory of God and the advancement of that holy cause of which I profess to be an unworthy disciple . . . how fervently do I desire to bring her [a sister] and my husband to the throne of peace and pleading only the shed blood of our Lord and Savior obtain pardon and redeeming love. . . .[19]

For many people what really mattered was the afterlife— what went on during the brief span of earthly life was merely preparation—and it required constant effort to avoid eternal damnation. Nor was it possible ever to rest assured that one was saved; the self-exhortation continued through life.

I am much too prone to allow the passing and vexatious scenes of this life to interrupt my religious enjoyments and for the time to impede my preparation for that life which is eternal. Oh My Divine Master, be pleased for the time to come to grant me Grace sufficient to help in every trying hour to overcome every evil propensity of my nature, so that I may be calm and collected at all times and ready . . . at a moment's notice . . . to depart in peace. . . .[20]

Another minister's wife put the matter much more succinctly: "I am not as much engaged in religion as I should be . . . . Too worldly." [21]

Occasionally piety might even be seen as a competitive accomplishment, as in the case of one bright young lady in Alabama who determined early in her life to become a missionary (and did, in fact, become Alabama's first woman missionary), who remarked, "I have established a reputation for piety and considerable intelligence. I am mortified when I hear of others doing better than I." [22] Often these women were cast into deep depression because they had slapped a child or whipped a slave. A woman who could hardly bear the sound of her husband tuning his violin gritted her teeth and said nothing, dedicated as she was to the ideal of self-sacrifice.[23] There was no rest for the conscience. "We owe it to our husbands, children and friends," wrote Caroline Merrick, "to represent as nearly as possible the ideal which they hold so dear. . . ." [24] "'Tis man's to act, 'tis woman's to endure," Caroline Hentz reflected in the midst of some of her more difficult trials with a husband she did not much respect and financial problems that were beyond her power to solve.[25] Women were made, Ella Thomas was sure, "to suffer and be strong." [26] "Give me a double portion of the grace of thy Spirit that I may learn *meekness* . . . ," wrote another.[27] "Your mother seems to brood much," wrote Joseph LeConte to his daughter.[28] "I looked into that young patient face and busy thought went far into the future," wrote a woman meditating upon her young daughter, "and all that women must here feel and suffer." [29] "The task of self-government was not easy," said Caroline Gilman.

To repress a harsh answer, to confess a fault, and to stop (right or wrong) in the midst of self-defence, in gentle submission, sometimes requires a struggle like life and death; but these *three* efforts are the golden threads with which domestic happiness is woven; once begin the fabric with this woof, and trials shall not break or sorrow tarnish it.

Men are not often unreasonable; their difficulties lie in not understanding the moral and physical structure of our sex. . . .

How clear it is, then, that woman loses by petulance and recrimination! Her first study must be self-control, almost to hypocrisy. A good wife must smile amid a thousand perplexities, and clear her voice to tones of cheerfulness when her frame is drooping with disease or else languish alone.[30]

Elizabeth Avery Meriwether stood practically alone among the diary keepers and memoirists when she asserted in her *Recollections of 92 Years* that at an early age she had rejected immortality on her own initiative. "It seemed to me preposterous to imagine that a *good* God would create a human being with the power to feel and to suffer if He knew before creating that being that it's fate was Hell for all eternity . . .—and I then came to the opinion I still hold, viz., that the Hell we mortals get is of our own making and that we get it on this earth and not in a future life." [31] Perhaps such independence of mind was of a piece with her decision to send all her husband's inherited slaves to Liberia.

Mrs. Meriwether along with a few sophisticated ladies of Charleston and New Orleans stand as exceptions. The overwhelming majority of southern women who have left records at all reveal their preoccupation with religion and its demands for self-denial. Women made up more than sixty percent of the membership lists of various churches.[32]

What function did these stern demands upon oneself for piety and goodness serve? In an uncertain world, full of change, economic insecurity, sudden death, did the search for perfection help to give some steady center to life? Certainly the constant reiteration of "God's will be done" helped to relieve the burden of understanding as well as the burden of dealing with recurrent crises. Observing the kinds of sudden disasters which were commonplace: the dry summer which destroyed a crop, the epidemic which killed a third of the slaves and half the children in the family, the sudden bankruptcy caused by external economic conditions, or by the simple generosity of having gone on

A7958.

someone else's note; the unexplained deaths of adolescents who were well and active one day and dead three days later; it is no wonder that a woman might feel herself to be not an actor but a pawn in some giant game she could not possibly understand. To assume it was all meaningless would be a prescription for insanity.

Perhaps, too, by being good one could make secret bargains with God or Fate. Yet the bargains didn't work, the children died anyway, health disappeared in spite of them, husbands were sometimes hardhearted or dissipated.

Perhaps the diaries are misleading. It may be that one way to manage fears and anxieties is to write them down, after which one can then go on to live a reasonably normal life. Some hint of this is contained in a huge collection preserved at the University of North Carolina wherein a woman's religious diary is as perfervid as any to be found, while her daily letters to sons away at school are matter-of-fact and down to earth, with only the normal amount of reference to salvation, church attendance, and the like.[33]

It seems possible that the demand for Christian perfection which so many women internalized, while it laid great burdens upon them also enabled the strongest to become truly remarkable mainstays of family life. The paradox is that the faith which sustained them added new burdens and increased the level of anxiety. Perhaps the vision of heaven was comforting (weary women often spoke of the longing for death and peace) but the price of admission was high. Here were excellent women, thousands of them, whose sins were of the most minor kind. Yet they carried constantly with them the conception of a jealous, wrathful God, capable of punishing by eternal damnation their innate corruption, whom they were yet supposed to love. Because of their understanding of what salvation required they were persuaded to apologize abjectly for the very qualities which make a woman (or a man for that matter) an interesting and rich personality—for spirit, for a roving mind, for pride to think well of themselves.

How this anxiety would have been resolved had there been no upheaval such as the Civil War it is impossible to know. But the war came, and self-abnegating southern women were put to sterner tests than they had previously imagined existed. With many men gone submissiveness was no longer a functional virtue. Once the war was over, slavery was also ended, and a new phase of women's relationship to the church began. In the on-rushing industrialization of the late nineteenth century many of the traditional economic tasks which women had performed in the recent rural past began to disappear. Even in the South, towns were multiplying and the urban population steadily increasing. The story is too familiar to require much repetition: smaller families, better health, canned food, store-bought clothes, all combined to reduce the time required for necessary household functions, and to expand the leisure time of urban wives. The presence of many Negro women willing—or compelled—to work for very low wages reduced still further the necessary tasks of many wives and mothers. Added to the economic facts was a certain psychological malaise, the key, perhaps, to much of the postwar development:

Women who had been fully occupied with the requirements of society and the responsibilities of a dependency of slaves, were now tossed to and fro amidst the exigencies and bewilderments of strange and for the most part painful circumstances, and were eager that new adjustments should relieve the strained situation, and that they might find out what to do.[34]

In direct contradiction to the old saw about Satan finding work for idle hands, it was the firm conviction of many women that if their families needed them less, the Lord had work for them to do. An energetic Alabama woman foreshadowed the future when she wrote Bishop James

Andrew in 1861, pointing to the immense amount of work southern women were then engaged upon, and saying that surely women loved God as much as country, if only the church would offer equally specific tasks to be done.

Here and there women's missionary societies had existed long before the war. At the first Baptist convention in Alabama in 1823, when Alabama was still a frontier, half of the small number of delegates present were sent by missionary societies, and "Stranger still, every one of these missionary societies was a little organization of women that had been formed in obscurity, none knowing of the existence of any other, and thus without concert of action." [35] A female missionary society in Columbus, Mississippi, was said to have had continuous existence from 1838, but before the war it always sent a man as its delegate to various conventions.[36] The records of these early societies are all but lost to history—and thus the societies themselves are only dimly remembered.

What came to pass in the 1870s was of a different order of magnitude. In that decade Methodist, Baptist, and Presbyterian women all over the South, released from the responsibilities of slaveholding and plantation administration, seemed to have received a simultaneous impulse which set them to organizing missionary societies, studying geography, raising money, and recruiting people to go to foreign shores.

The prevailing doctrine of these churches with respect to women was extremely conservative. Church publications were full of praise for ladylike women, and expressions of horror at "unsexed" females. The erudite *Quarterly Review* of the Methodist Episcopal Church South examined the question "May Women Preach?" and stood firmly with St. Paul who was presumed to have forbidden it.

So in Sunday-schools and Bible classes, and Missionary Societies, great caution is needed—more, perhaps, than is always shown—in utilizing the gifts and graces of pious, zealous, and intelligent women. Nothing can compensate for the sacrifice of feminine modesty: this must be guarded, though the heavens fall! [37]

Baptists editors agreed completely, nor did their opinions change much with the passing of decades. In 1868 the Baptist *Religious Herald* asserted:

As the rival of man, in the struggle for place, power and prominence, she, as the "weaker vessel," is doomed to defeat. From such a contest, she must inevitably come forth, not with modesty, delicacy and loveliness which impart a charm and influence to her sex, but soiled, dishonored and disappointed.[38]

Thirty-one years later the same paper was saying:

When . . . woman becomes *emancipated* from the care of the young and the making of the home, she has entered into the worst of all bondage, which comes always to every one who disregards the law of his own life. They only "walk at liberty" who have learned to obey the divine precepts, as written in their being.[39]

Within the church itself Baptist men were very slow to grant new privileges to women. There, too, St. Paul's injunction to "let the women keep silent in churches" was sternly applied.

We do not propose to be persuaded, cajoled, or drawn by the force of public or private opinion, into adopting this unscriptural and foolish practice. . . . Let *all* our people *positively* refuse the use of our churches to such an unscriptural and dangerous innovation. . . . "From womanly men, and from manly women, good Lord deliver us." [40]

The Baptist church maintained an even more conservative stance vis-à-vis its women than did the Methodist. Baptist ministers firmly opposed any southwide women's

104

organization for fear it would become a front for danger-ous feminism. "An independent organization of women," wrote the Reverend Tiberius Jones of Virginia, "naturally tends toward a violation of divine interdict against a wom-an's becoming a public religious teacher." [41] It was 1888 before Baptist women were strong enough to insist on their right to a southwide organization, but in the mean-time they carried on within their missionary societies the same kinds of programs—and the same kind of self-develop-ment—as their Methodist sisters.

It was no wonder that one Mississippi Baptist woman, praying for the enlightenment of the heathen added to her prayer "I pray God to enlighten the minds of our benighted husbands, and show them their error." [42]

Yet these same Baptists, while officially opposing wom-en's rights in any form, encouraged the expanding role of women in benevolent causes and encouraged participation in the temperance crusade "as long as these efforts remain dissociated from the feminist agitation and politics." [43]

The Methodists, too, were happy to turn over to women not only the responsibility for raising money for foreign missions, but responsibility for furnishing and taking care of parsonages and for local philanthropy. In meeting these responsibilities the women began to revise their self-image and ultimately found themselves to be part of the feminist movement which the church so deplored. In due course they would begin to demand more power within the church itself. The church fathers were not as foresighted as a certain antebellum minister who had refused permission for a woman's prayer meeting on the ground that if women were alone "who knows what they would pray for?"

The tendency of women to form themselves into reli-gious societies was present in all the denominations. The introspective piety of the early decades of the century turned outward, the desire to do good in society increased, and a missionary spirit directed both to foreign lands and to social problems closer to home developed very rapidly.

Groups of women had hardly begun to realize that their own experience was being duplicated in many places when they began to think of setting up a southwide organization. The Methodists were first to achieve this goal. In 1878 the Methodist General Conference, after some debate, authorized a Woman's Board of Foreign Missions, and at the close of its first year of existence the Board counted 218 societies, 5,890 members, four thousand dollars in the treasury, and one missionary in China. Ten years later there were 2,399 societies, 56,783 members, and missionaries in dozens of places. The women were learning to administer programs and to handle large sums of money. By 1890 the Methodist Woman's Board of Foreign Missions owned almost two hundred thousand dollars' worth of property, and had responsibility for ten boarding schools, thirty-one day schools, and a hospital.[44] Three years later the organization had grown to seventy-six thousand members. Actual service in foreign lands offered a new form of work for women and a new opportunity for women whose religious zeal did not find adequate outlets at home.

While saving the heathen had a very strong emotional appeal, one which returning missionaries developed fully, women in the missionary societies were also becoming aware of needs nearer home.

In the process of carrying out what appeared on the surface to be rather traditional philanthropic work among the poorer people, church women came into direct contact with social problems which led them to a new interest in home missionary work, so great that some leaders worried for fear the foreign missions would be neglected. As early as 1882 Miss Laura Haygood organized the Trinity Home Mission of Atlanta, having for its purpose the "physical, mental, and moral elevation of the poor of the city, and especially of our own Church and congregation." By the end of the first year this society had established an industrial school and a home for dependent and helpless women.[45]

Southern church women were observing, as many of their secular counterparts in the northern settlement-house movement had observed, the social consequences of industrial development. In Chicago the most obvious victims of the factory were foreign immigrants; in the South they were poor white people. In 1899 the general secretary of the Methodist Board of Home Missions told her sisters that they were standing on the threshold of a great opportunity as the southern states began to develop manufacturing. She called upon them to be farsighted, to move at once "to ameliorate existing conditions, to see that laws to protect helpless childhood are created and enforced. . . ." [46] By 1908 local church women were studying industrial relations in their regular meetings, and passing resolutions of concern. The concern did not stop with resolutions but issued in a widespread network of settlement houses in industrial communities.[47]

In 1899 Southern Methodist women took the first tentative steps toward corporate concern with the problems of black people. In 1900 the Women's Missionary Council urged women throughout the South to "do all in their power in their own communities to help and uplift the Negro race," and a year later the council began to raise money to add an annex for girls to the Paine Institute, a school which the Methodist Church had established in Augusta, Georgia, to train Negro leaders. Ten years later a young Alabama woman, Mary DeBardelben, began her missionary work, not in a foreign land, but in a Negro settlement house in Augusta.

Meantime the Methodist women established a Bureau of Social Service with Mrs. J. D. Hammond as its superintendent. Mrs. Hammond, whose husband later became president of Paine Institute, published in 1914 a book called *In Black and White* which laid out a program for

ameliorating the conditions of southern Negroes. Read in
the context of its year of publication, and with the realization that the author was a southern woman whose parents
had been slaveowners, the book is an astonishing document.
Social equality aside, Mrs. Hammond tackled nearly every
hard problem which vexed race relations in the South. She
announced that she did not believe Negroes to be inferior.
In her cosmos God had put them on earth, even as he had
white people, to fulfill some destiny. In a series of hard-
hitting chapters, she held a mirror to southern society
which must have caused some soul searching among such of
her readers as did not throw the book away in disgust.
Taking her stand firmly on the Christian ethic, she casti-
gated her fellow white southerners for permitting Negro
slums, for sending youngsters to jail whose home experience
had prepared them for nothing but delinquency, for permitting inequity in the courts of law, for accepting stinking
Jim Crow cars, for failing to educate talent when it came
in a black skin, for failing to set an example of honesty and
fair dealing, for hypocrisy and insensitivity.[48] The book
provided a blueprint for much of the work which would
develop in the twenties under the leadership of a group
calling itself the Commission on Inter-racial Cooperation,
headed by Will Alexander.

Among the three leading Protestant denominations,
women in the Methodist Church moved furthest in the
direction of a social gospel. It is also noticeable that many
of the women who led secular reform movements in the
South were members of the Methodist Church. The reasons
for this are not clear, though some speculations are possible. Connectionalism was a Methodist concept. Unlike the
Baptists, who were congregational in church government,
the Methodists had a higher layer of organization, which
meant not only that the experience of joint decision-making
existed in that church but also that members of various
conferences could sometimes move beyond what members

of local church groups might have sanctioned. This pattern, as we have seen, was reflected in the fact that the Methodist women had a southwide missionary organization somewhat earlier than the Baptists. Further, the Methodists had a good communication network—the publishing house was founded before 1800.

Wesleyan theology tended toward a this-worldiness, and emphasis on doing good here and now. The evangelical denominations shared certain concerns, but Methodist women seem to have reached out ahead of the others in matters such as child labor reform, prison reform, and especially in the effort to improve race relations.[49]

The mushrooming of women's organizations in the churches had consequences quite beyond the number of missionaries supported, schools founded, hospitals inaugurated in foreign lands, or even the social settlements closer home. Church work was the essential first step in the emancipation of thousands of southern women from their antebellum image of themselves and of "woman's sphere." In 1879 a prominent North Carolina minister assured his daughter that membership in a missionary society would be "no compromise of female modesty and refinement," [50] and no doubt many other men gave the same assurance. What these admirers of ladylike women did not foresee were the psychological consequences of the missionary society experience. The historians of South Carolina Presbyterianism remarked that at the beginning the women in the missionary society were so shy that they contented themselves with reciting the Lord's Prayer in unison. From this they progressed to sentence prayers, delivered seriatim, and finally (they triumphantly noted) sixty percent were prepared to lead the prayer! [51] It was said that a statewide meeting of the South Carolina Methodist Women's Missionary Society was the first public meeting in the state to be presided over by a woman—this in 1880. "With experience and a growing and compelling sense of mission women in the church began to gain confidence and slowly emerge from the self-consciousness and fear which had bound them," observed the historian of Methodist women.[52] The public life of virtually every Southern woman leader for forty years began in a church society. "The struggle that it cost the women to attain to the ultimate goal, in satisfaction of a conviction that the right was theirs to labor for the Lord, only served to qualify them the more for greater success, when once the end sought was reached," concluded the historian of the Alabama Baptists.[53]

As women gained self-confidence and felt pride in their achievements they began to push harder for independence and greater rights within the church structure. A bitter battle took place in the Methodist Church in 1906, when, without consulting the women who had built both organizations, the men in the General Conference decided to combine the Foreign and Home Missionary Societies, and put them under the control of a male-dominated Board of Missions. One woman missionary was so incensed that she resigned forever from the Methodist Church, though she continued her work.

As late as 1910 one worried Methodist woman was writing to another that she feared the women would "lose their independence of thought when they lost responsibility for, and management of their own affairs .... I fear the future will see the most intelligent women seeking a field of usefulness elsewhere and leave the less intelligent lacking the leadership that leads to enthusiasm and fuller development. ... We are in a helpless minority in a body where the membership is largely made up of men opposed to independence of thought in women." [54] From long experience the women decided they had no choice but to keep their tempers and try again. Finally, after repeated rebuffs, Methodist women were granted laity rights—in 1918.[55] In spite of, perhaps in part because of, the difficulties they encountered women learned in the churches to be leaders. As individual women developed purpose and capacity and were frustrated in their plans by unsympathetic males, they came more and more to desire independence, and to take responsibility for their own thinking.

In the meantime another development, which sprang from somewhat the same sources as the women's missionary societies, was the rapid growth of the Woman's Christian Temperance Union. In the early eighties Frances Willard, the extraordinary national president of the W.C.T.U., made the first of a series of southern forays. In New Orleans in 1881 she addressed a large audience in the Carondelet Methodist Church. A year later she returned and drafted Caroline Merrick, wife of a prominent judge, to be president of the New Orleans W.C.T.U. Mrs. Merrick thought temperance a thankless reform, but she found herself unable to refuse Miss Willard, who, she thought, had done more than any other person in the nineteenth century to "widen the outlook and develop the mental aspirations" of women.[56] Thereafter Mrs. Merrick spent ten years as president of the organization, and as a result was said to have been the first woman in Louisiana to speak in public on public questions.[57]

In 1883 a "few brave souls" summoned a convention of Christian women in North Carolina, and with Miss Willard's aid launched the union in that state. Six years later the scene was Jackson, Mississippi, where Frances Willard drafted a woman, who had not until that moment known of the organization's existence, to become an organizer. Belle Kearney, the woman in question, felt after prayerful meditation that she had heard God's call; in any case she had heard the call of Frances Willard.

Miss Willard's astonishing personal effectiveness was one reason the W.C.T.U. spread so rapidly in the South. A southern woman who later became prominent in national work said that "The first time I heard her I lay awake all night for sheer gladness. It was such a wonderful revelation to me that a woman like Miss Willard could exist. I thanked God and took courage for humanity." [58]

It is clear from the publications of the southern W.C.T.U. that many women had fastened upon alcohol as the root cause of a number of related things that bothered them about southern men and southern life, and in their fanatic insistence upon its eradication (even to the point of advertising flavoring in crystal form to avoid the alcoholic solvent, and of eschewing brandy in puddings) they managed—at this remove—to make themselves and their cause quite ridiculous. To see them as a joke is to miss the point.

Drinking was then virtually a male prerogative. It had long been a significant part of the life of many southern men. While temperance as a cause dated back to the 1830s, temperance as a practice was not widespread among antebellum men. Eliza Frances Andrews, editing her Civil War diary for publication in the 1890's, commented in the preface:

In fact, I have been both surprised and shocked in reading over this story of a by-gone generation, to see how prevalent was the use of wines and other alcoholic liquors, and how lightly an occasional over-indulgence was regarded. In this respect there can be no doubt that the world has changed greatly for the better. When "gentlemen" . . . were staying in the house, it was a common courtesy to place a bottle of wine, or brandy, or both, with the proper adjuncts, in the room of each guest, so that he might help himself to a "night-cap" on going to bed, or an "eye opener" before getting up in the morning. . . .[59]

Miss Andrews' reminiscence is borne out by the sentimental fiction of the antebellum years which is filled with drunken husbands (only discovered to be such after marriage) and disillusioned wives. In the social circles somewhat less exalted than that of the Andrews family the frontier's rough-and-ready pleasure in hard drink was widespread, a fact recognized by the evangelical churches which early began to preach temperance as necessary to salvation. The war appeared to have killed the temperance societies and to have fostered the drink habit. Observers thought that social drinking and tippling were prevalent everywhere in Reconstruction, and such things as the rise of commercial villages and the multiplication of country stores made alcohol more accessible. Drinking was thought to have been stimulated, too, by the despondency with which the future was regarded. Saturday afternoons were scenes of alcoholic confusion in many villages.[60] The Negroes, whose access to hard drink had been carefully regulated in slavery, were now able to join their white brothers in weekend orgies, though some observers thought them less given to drunkenness than white men. For both races there was an intimate relationship between alcohol and crime, particularly violent crime.

Such behavior was troublesome to women for a number of reasons—not only because it seemed to lead to a threatening social instability, but because it led to hardship in many individual families. In antebellum days much had been made by men and women alike of the power of "woman's influence" to bring men, not naturally so inclined, to virtuous habits. But "influence" was a chancy tool at best, and even a casual student of personality psychology would guess that it often worked in ways quite remote from the goal of the person trying to exert the influence. Total abstinence pledges and statewide prohibition were more likely to be effective, or at least it was possible to hope so.

There was also a strain of crusading revivalism in the organization which may have appealed to some women whose churches forbade them the privilege of preaching. In this wholly female organization women could, and did, preach—though perhaps not from a pulpit.

The union women did not stop with prohibition and total abstinence. They soon developed a broad educational program on the physiological effects of alcohol and went to work to make its teaching mandatory in the schools. This was the beginning of a good deal of public school teaching of health education. The W.C.T.U. may well have been the first group in the South to speak openly of the need for sex education.

An interest in prison reform and the demand for juvenile reformatories also grew directly from women's work with alcoholics among convicts. Mrs. L. C. Blair of the Raleigh, North Carolina, W.C.T.U. told a state legislative committee in 1905:

As superintendent of prison work for the W.C.T.U. I have for ten years studied this subject in our county jails and state prisons, and if I had time and language to portray to you, sirs, the dreadful effects I have seen arising from our methods of dealing with youthful criminals, I would have but little doubt of getting a reform school. . . .[61]

In 1889 Mrs. Sallie Chapin, a talented Charleston aristocrat, was president of the South Carolina W.C.T.U. and spoke to the annual convention. In the course of her speech she referred to the convict lease system ("a disgrace to the civilization of the nineteenth century"), to a plan for educating mothers and reducing infant mortality, to the concern she felt for reducing the normal work week of laboring men. Discussion at the same convention revealed the fact that the Spartanburg Union was running a woman's exchange to aid women who needed to earn a living.

The notion of the W.C.T.U. as in part an organization motivated by a desire to control male behavior is borne out by the emphasis its members put on what they called "social purity," the accepted euphemism for elimination of venereal disease. One approach to eliminating venereal disease was to attack that ancient bogey of women—the double standard.

Like the women in the churches the women in the W.C.T.U. in many cases underwent a personal transformation, as they learned to think for themselves, organize programs, assume leadership; as they met—in national conventions—women from other parts of the United States. Belle Kearney was a case in point. In the first year of her "ministry" she traveled all over Mississippi and organized hundreds of unions among young women and children. She held business meetings and discussed the methods of work best suited to forward the interest of the societies she was organizing. In 1889 she went to a national convention in Chicago and gained, she said, "a new vision of woman's life." [62]

Mrs. Lide Meriwether of Memphis, Tennessee, who had been born in 1829, recorded of herself that after the war she lived a simple home life, devoted to husband and children. Then, when "most women are only waiting to die, their children reared and the tasks of the spirit largely ended, began for her a life of new thought and activity." A friend in Arkansas asked her to help in a W.C.T.U. convention, where she discovered an hitherto unrecognized talent for public speaking. Under her leadership the Tennessee W.C.T.U. grew and flourished, and from this work she was led into an even more ardent interest in woman suffrage. [63]

Like the church women these women were also by their choice of subjects brought into direct contact with many of the social problems of their communities, and decided that they could and should do something about them. Because they wanted temperance education in the schools and prohibition for their states they found themselves, willy-nilly, in politics. The frustration they felt when members of legislatures listened politely and voted as they pleased led W.C.T.U. women to become the earliest southern suffragists.

They see the solution of the drink problem lies to a great extent in woman's ballot; and, looking deeper, they find that the key to the whole situation. Not only in political and philanthropic circles have women been brought to realize these restrictions, but in ecclesiastical as well.[64]

One theme running through the essays in this volume is that of religion reinforcing southern culture. Looked at through women's lives the theme becomes more complex. The antebellum church by its doctrines reinforced the most limited and restricted role for women while it also provided a source of personal strength. The postwar church, still preaching Paul's doctrine that women should be silent in the churches and holding firmly to the antebellum image of the southern lady, inadvertently provided Christian women with a road to emancipation. Timothy Smith has argued that in the United States generally the revivalism of the early nineteenth century laid the foundation for social reform. While Southerners took part in some aspects of the prewar reform movement, the presence of slavery and the link between reform and abolitionism often worked to limit practical applications of Christian perfection to the antebellum society.

Furthermore, while slavery existed many southern women of the class discussed here were fully occupied with what could legitimately be called the extended family of the plantation. Not only their own children and relatives, but all the slaves were their responsibility, and if there was one thing no plantation mistress complained of it was not being needed.

Emancipation at one stroke pushed many Southerners for the first time into a nuclear family. The economic stringency of the immediate postwar period reduced the amount of social visiting and perhaps even of kinship responsibilities. It was precisely when these old functions were disappearing that women in all the evangelical denominations began to develop their intense interest in foreign missions, and then in reform closer to home. In the beginning they used the institution most familiar to them, in which they felt most at ease—the church. The W.C.T.U. was almost a church, and it was only after two decades of experience with these familiar institutions that the more innovative women's clubs and suffrage societies began to appear.

The study of southern religion has assumed, as is customary among American historians, that men spoke for the whole society. Even the fragmentary evidence here is enough to make it clear that women had their own voice, though possibly its tone concealed its substance. Much more work must be done before it will be possible to say how many southern women were actually involved in serious social reform. Certainly there were some. Southern women cheered Frances Willard enthusiastically when, speaking in Atlanta in 1890, she announced that the wage system was certain to pass away, that labor unions were the hope of the future, and urged upon industry a consideration of profit sharing. "If to teach this is to be a socialist," Miss Willard had said, "then so let it be." [65] It might be difficult to find an assemblage of southern men of the same social class and economic status cheering, or even listening to, such a speech at that time.

If the degree of female radicalism needs more study, one other thing is inescapably clear. Whatever function they served initially, the missionary societies and the W.C.T.U. (and the women's clubs and suffrage organizations for which they paved the way) provided a school for women leaders of considerable significance in the shaping of southern society and even southern politics in the ensuing decades.

NOTES

1. Sidney Mead, *The Lively Experiment* (New York: Harper, 1963), p. 92.

2. Thomas Nelson Page, *Social Life in Old Virginia*, (New York: Charles Scribner's Sons, 1898), pp. 38-42.

3. Diary of Myra Smith, 17 April 1851, Sommerville-Howorth Papers, Schlesinger Library, Radcliffe College, Cambridge, Mass.

4. Smith Diary, January 1852.

5. Diary of Fannie Moore Webb Bumpas, 5 March 1842, Southern Historical Collection, University of North Carolina, Chapel Hill. Hereafter cited as SHC, UNC.

6. Diary of Charlotte Beatty, 1843, SHC, UNC.

7. Sarah Wadley Journal, 4 February 1863, SHC, UNC. She was eighteen at the time!

8. Lucilla McCorkle Diary, May 1846, SHC, UNC.

9. Lizzie Smith to R. L. Felton, 22 June 1876. Felton Papers, University of Georgia, Athens.

10. Annie to Lollie, 14 December 1859, in Lucy Cole Burwell Papers, Duke University Manuscript Department, Durham, N. C. Cited hereafter as Duke.

11. E. G. Thomas Diary, 8 April, 1855, Duke.

12. Jer. 17:9.

13. Lucilla McCorkle Diary, SHC, UNC.

14. *Ebb Tide*, as seen through the Diary of Josephine Clay Habersham, Spencer B. King, Jr., ed. (Athens: University of Georgia Press, 1958), pp. 103-4.

15. *Ibid.*, p. 77.

16. Wadley Journal, 20 August 1863, SHC, UNC.

17. Diary of Mrs. Isaac Hilliard, 21 April 1850, Louisiana State University Department of Archives, Baton Rouge, La. Cited hereafter as LSU.

18. Smith Diary, 15 December 1850.

19. Thomas Diary, 8 April 1855.

20. Diary of Anne Beale Davis, August 14, 1842, SHC, UNC.

21. Bumpas Diary, 26 June 1842.

22. Martha Foster Crawford Diary, 1850, Duke.

23. Thomas Diary, 30 November 1858.

24. To "my dear friend," 23 May 1857, LSU.

25. Diary, 5 March 1836, SHC, UNC.

26. Diary, New Year's Day 1859, Duke.

27. McCorkle Diary, 12 July 1846, SHC, UNC.

28. Joseph LeConte to Emma, 25 April 1869, LeConte Papers, SHC, UNC.

29. Beatty Diary, 21 March 1843.

30. *Caroline Gilman, Recollections of a Southern Matron* (New York: Harper and Brothers, 1838), p. 256.

31. Elizabeth Avery Meriwether, *Recollections of 92 Years* (Nashville: Tennessee Historical Society, 1958), p. 35.

32. This estimate is based on a study of membership lists of over a hundred churches made by Professor Donald Mathews of the University of North Carolina.

33. Beale-Davis Papers, SHC, UNC.

34. Caroline E. Merrick, *Old Time in Dixie Land* (New York: Grafton Press, 1901), p. 172.

35. B. F. Riley, A *Memorial History of the Baptists of Alabama* (Philadelphia: Judson Press, 1923), pp. 35-36.

36. Z. T. Leavell and T. J. Bailey, A *Complete History of Mississippi Baptists,* Vol. II (Jackson: Mississippi Baptist Publishing Co., 1904), p. 415.

37. July (1881) 478-88.

38. February 20 (1868) 2.

39. January 5 (1899) 1.

40. *Biblical Recorder* (Raleigh, North Carolina, 10 February

1892, p. 2, quoted in Rufus B. Spain, *At Ease in Zion* (Nashville: Vanderbilt University Press, 1967), p. 169.

41. "Minutes of Virginia Baptist Association 1888," p. 42.

42. Leavell and Bailey, *Mississippi Baptists,* p. 1417.

43. Spain, *Zion,* p. 168.

44. *Twelfth Annual Report,* Woman's Board of Foreign Missions, Methodist Episcopal Church, South (Nashville: The Methodist Publishing House, 1891).

45. Noreen Dunn Tatum, *Crown of Service* (Nashville: Parthenon Press, 1960), p. 26.

46. *Ibid.,* p. 349.

47. *Ibid.,* pp. 352-53. For general background see Broadus Mitchell, *Rise of Cotton Mills in the South* (Baltimore: Johns Hopkins University, 1921).

48. Lily H. Hammond, *In Black and White* (New York, 1914).

49. See Anne Firor Scott, *The Southern Lady* (Chicago: University of Chicago Press, 1970), pp. 135-63, and *passim,* for the secular reformers. In gathering evidence about women reformers I began to notice the disproportionate number of Methodists. Careful statistical studies need to be made to check this impression. Various theologically trained friends have helped me speculate about the possible causes; especially Professor Thomas Langford of the Duke University department of religion, and Professor Samuel Hill, the editor of this volume.

50. A. W. Plyler, *The Iron Duke of the Methodist Itinerancy* (Nashville: Cokesbury Press, 1925), p. 166.

51. F. D. Jones and W. H. Mills, eds., *History of the Presbyterian Church in South Carolina Since 1850* (Columbia, 1926), p. 442.

52. Tatum, *Crown,* p. 37.

53. B. F. Riley, *Memorial History,* p. 164.

54. Mary Helm to Nellie Nugent Somerville, Somerville Papers, Schlesinger Library, Radcliffe College, Cambridge, Mass.

55. Tatum, *Crown,* pp. 34-40.

56. Merrick, *Old Times,* pp. 143-45.

57. Obituary in New Orleans *Times-Picayune,* 30 March 1908.

58. Quoted in Anna A. Gordon, *The Life of Frances Willard* (Evanston: Lakeside Press, 1912), p. 102.

59. Eliza Frances Andrews, *Wartime Journal of a Georgia Girl* (New York: D. Appleton, 1908), pp. 7-8.

60. Francis B. Simkins and Robert H. Woody, *Reconstruction in South Carolina* (Chapel Hill: University of North Carolina Press, 1938), pp. 322 ff.

61. *North Carolina White Ribbon,* 1906.

62. Belle Kearney, *A Slaveholder's Daughter* (New York, 1900), pp. 167-68.

63. Frances Willard and Mary A. Livermore, *American Women* (New York: Mast, Crowell and Kirkpatrick, 1897), Vol. II, p. 499.

64. Kearney, *Daughter,* p. 174.

65. Address by Frances E. Willard to the Seventeenth Convention of the W.C.T.U., Atlanta, 1890.

5
THE STRUCTURE OF A FUNDAMENTALIST CHRISTIAN BELIEF-SYSTEM

Southern Protestants are universally said to be fundamentalists, and fundamentalist is generally defined as a person who believes in a literal interpretation of the Bible. However, a moment's reflection exposes a defect in this definition. It is, simply stated, that in the past many southern Protestants were illiterate; some are illiterate today. One would indeed be surprised to find illiterate people making literacy a prerequisite for access to their system of religious belief. This surely cannot be the case. As evidence to the contrary, Samuel Hill has pointed out that even in their seminaries southern Protestants have a rather shallow sense of history and a somewhat undeveloped tradition of theological scholarship.[1]

What, then, are the essential ingredients of fundamentalism? In 1961, as a graduate student in anthropology at the University of North Carolina, I did research on the world view of some rural-born, working-class, southern white people, and discovered what I think is a partial answer to this question.[2] As my informants explained their beliefs to me, it became more and more striking that although they said that they believed in the literal truth of the Bible, they almost never referred to the Bible when explaining their beliefs, choosing instead to draw examples from everyday life. Although they were literate, the belief-system they used to interpret events in their lives could have been transmitted from one generation to another solely through oral modes of communication.[3]

In good anthropological fashion, I worked with a deliberately cultivated sense of estrangement, trying to look at my informants' beliefs as an outsider would. From this vantage point, it became increasingly obvious that their belief-system had a peculiar structure, utilizing the principles of fate and supernatural justice in a closed, exceptionless structure. Though differing in detail, the overall shape of the fundamentalist Christian belief-system is unmistakably similar to that of belief-systems in nonwestern societies.[4] It will not be amiss to justify this last statement at some length.

As religious or ethical principles, fate and supernatural justice are contradictory by ordinary logical standards. When a person is said to be the victim of fate, his moral standing is irrelevant; fate, an amoral principle, attacks good and bad alike. In contrast, supernatural justice is a moral principle; when a person is said to have suffered from supernatural justice, his failure to uphold moral norms is given as the reason for his misfortune.

Meyer Fortes, a social anthropologist specializing in African cultures, has attempted to show that both of these principles occur side by side in the religious beliefs of West African peoples, particularly the Tallensi.[5] In Tale society the social groups of greatest functional importance for the individual are a series of progressively inclusive kinship groups. Consistent with this, their religious system has as its principal deities ancestral spirits. Fortes makes it clear that a Tale individual's relationships with his ancestral spirits are patterned on his relationships with living kinsmen. Events in his life which are caused by ancestral spirits are clearly within the realm of supernatural justice; these events are the consequences of "social" relationships governed by explicit, well-known rules. In small-scale societies, the life histories of individuals are similar in many respects, and a large portion of what happens in their lives can consequently be explained in terms of supernatural justice.

At the same time, however, individuals have their peculiarities in all societies, and while most people fit acceptably into prescribed social roles, some are misfits. Here, argues Fortes, is where the principle of fate or destiny comes in. Before a person is born, the Tallensi believe that his soul asks for what he wants out of life and that this determines his destiny. It sometimes happens that a person's soul rejects what the Tallensi define as the good things in life, and the person consequently has a bad destiny. Later in life, such a person may meticuously meet all his ritual obligations to his ancestors, but experience one misfortune after another. Since this bad destiny is beyond a person's consciousness, he can discover its existence only by consulting a diviner, and he can then attempt to change it with the diviner's help, though not all such attempts are successful.

Fortes has been challenged on his use of supernatural justice and fate as a "paradigm" for analyzing Tale beliefs, but what is more relevant for my purpose here is his observation that both principles seem to occur together in many theistic western and oriental religions.[6] My research indicates that the two principles do indeed occur in at least one variety of theistic western religion, namely in the belief-system of fundamentalist Protestants in the South.

The parallel between the fundamentalist Christian belief-system and belief-systems in nonwestern societies raises an important problem.[7] Like many nonwestern belief-systems, the fundamentalist Christian belief-system contains a basic contradiction. It says on the one hand that virtuous people will be rewarded and evil people punished through supernatural justice, and on the other hand that virtuous people may suffer and evil people prosper through the workings of fate. Stated in these terms, we may ask how anyone could possibly believe in such a self-canceling world view. As we shall presently see, the contradiction between supernatural justice and fate is central to the fundamentalist Christian belief-system, but it does not weaken the system; indeed, this contradiction is largely responsible for the enormous generality of the system.

In the pages which follow we shall first examine the elemental causal agencies postulated in this belief-system; next we shall consider certain principles which link these agencies to events in the everyday world; and finally we shall briefly consider how these agencies and principles articulate with people in their transit through the social structure. It should be pointed out that I shall be using the notion of structure in two distinct senses: in the sense of the structure of beliefs, a fundamentally nontemporal, logical kind of structure, and in the sense of the structure of action, a fundamentally temporal kind of structure.

I

The fundamentalist Christian belief-system postulates the existence of three elemental causal agencies: "God," the "Devil," and the "mind." [8] Though it is somehow tempting to conceptualize these agencies as a kind of triangle, this is not the case. They can more appropriately be imagined as a chain of communication in which the mind is the link between God and the Devil. Also, retaining our chain of communication analogy, we shall presently see that God and the mind are in a kind of asymmetrical, two-way communication, while the Devil is in one-way communication with the mind.

God is a somewhat personalized spiritual being who is believed to be the ultimate cause of everything. Although all things and events can, through linked causes, be traced back to God, he is not the proximate cause of everything. That is, although God shaped the fundamental structure of the universe, the constituent elements in this structure operate with some autonomy. As one of my informants put it, "God has a hand in everything."

Thus, one of the causal agencies in this belief-system is thought to have shaped the nature of the other two. The mind, my informants said, is a gift that God gives to each individual. I neglected to explicitly ask my informants whether God created the Devil, but I rather think they would say he did. More importantly, they would say that God determined the nature of the relationship that now exists between them; that is, because of God's rather drastic course of action they are no longer on speaking terms.

My informants said that God is aware of everything a person does or thinks and that he works from the "inside" and from the "outside." What this means is that God makes his presence known to people from the inside through "conscience" or "feeling." The conscience is closely related to the mind, but I did not collect enough information to indicate the precise nature of the relationship. Furthermore, he can make his presence and intentions known to people directly, from the outside, by causing events in peoples' lives and by communicating with them through "signs" and "warnings." We shall examine signs and warnings in more detail later; here, we should only note that while people communicate with God through ritual and through ordinary language, God communicates with people through an ambiguous "language" of symbolic events. That is, the meaning of God's communication is not directly apprehended, as one apprehends the meaning of spoken words; it must, as we shall see, be interpreted contemplatively. Thus, while God and the mind are in two-way communication, these are two distinctly different modes of communication.

I should point out here that in the past my principal informants occasionally attended a church in which the members "spoke in unknown tongues." Thus they are aware of a belief that God, through the agency of people in paranormal or ecstatic states of mind, is able to communicate through the medium of language, albeit a language that is unknown and presumed ancient. It is difficult to say whether this belief is a part of my informants' belief-system. They are aware of it, and they do not definitely say that it is a wrong or erroneous belief, but it does not seem to occupy a prominent place in their active beliefs. Even if it did, it would not alter the character of the beliefs they do hold. Speaking in unknown tongues, like signs and warnings, is a mode of communication that must be interpreted contemplatively.

The Devil is a personalized agency who is believed to work from the inside only. Unlike God, the Devil cannot cause events in a person's life, nor can he communicate as directly with the mind as God can. Furthermore, my informants never suggested that people communicate in any way with the Devil.[9]

The Devil works from the inside; indeed, he may be said to be "in" a person. The Devil influences a person through "feelings" or "temptations." That is, temptation is not essentially a cognitive phenomenon, but rather a feeling that one has when faced with a moral choice. When one yields to temptation, one is inevitably led into immorality. Furthermore, unlike God, the Devil is not aware of everything a person is thinking. This preserves the partial autonomy of the mind.

The last of the three agencies, the mind, is said to be a gift from God. More properly, it is a propensity which God gives to each individual. My informants said that a newly born infant "has no mind." That is, the mind is something that develops with age. Subsequently, we shall see that the dynamic relationships between God, the mind, and the Devil change as the mind develops. This, of course, indicates that the three agencies participate in the same system and cannot be understood apart from the system.

My informants distinguished between "strong minds" and "weak minds," with weak mind roughly meaning congenital or acquired psychophysical defects. Surprisingly, they felt that all strong minds are roughly equivalent; although they have some awareness of modern notions of intelligence and aptitude, mainly through the tests their children take in school, these concepts have no intrinsic position in their belief-system.

The mind is simply the place where an individual's knowledge and memories reside; it allows him to be aware of the world, and it enables him to make decisions. Aside from strength or normalcy, the most important mental qualities are "faith" and "willpower." Faith is the quality which enables a person to have confidence in ultimately good outcomes without regard to past or present outcomes. Willpower is the ability to strive and to resist temptation.

II

Now that we have examined the elemental causal agencies, it remains for us to examine the kinds of events which this belief-system must explain and the principles by means of which explanation is accomplished. According to my analysis, the belief-system recognizes three major classes of events: *meaningless events, meaningful events,* and an intermediate class of *ambiguous events* which are meaningful to some but meaningless to others, depending upon their ritual condition. The major explanatory principles are *fate* and *supernatural justice.* In addition, the belief-system recognizes a variety of subsidiary principles such as *choice, skill, accident,* and so on.[10]

	MEANINGFUL EVENTS		AMBIGUOUS EVENTS	MEANINGLESS EVENTS
	Bad Events	Good Events		
Bad People	Super-natural Justice	Fate	Signs & Warnings	Choice, Skill, Accident, Etc.
Good People	Fate	Super-natural Justice		

Figure 1

Although my informants would say that *all* events are meaningful if one only searches for their meaning, this merely means that all events are ultimately linked to God, if one only takes the trouble to trace out the chains of causation. In practice, however, many events—probably most of the events a person experiences—need not be interpreted. Many events, for example, flow from the simple exercise of choice. A man simply chooses to buy a Ford instead of a Plymouth. The act of choosing and buying a particular car is enormously important in terms of the secular values of working-class white Southerners.[11] Secular values aside, the act of buying a particular car is meaningless from the standpoint of the belief-system.

The consequences of disobeying certain social norms are likewise meaningless. For example, when someone gets a ticket for illegal parking, no interpretation is required. Other events may be explained in terms of skill. Skill is acquired by learning, and some men obviously have more of it than others. Thus, if a newly installed roof leaks, it may simply mean that the carpenter who installed it was not sufficiently skilled. In addition, my informants explained many events as accidents. A man spills coffee on his shirt, nicks himself while shaving, or runs over a dog while driving to work. In general, though, accident explains only those events which are trivial from the standpoint of a person's social well-being. The major events in life, the socially important events, are never accountable in terms of accident.

The major events in life—particularly those involving success, failure, illness, healing, and death—are meaningful events. These are events which are explained by the two fundamental principles of the belief-system: supernatural justice and fate. Supernatural justice, an eminently moral principle, is wholly consistent with the basic nature of society and culture: with superb simplicity, the principle affirms that conformity to social norms is rewarded while deviance is punished. Men, through the agency of their minds, are able to choose. Some men choose in accordance with prevailing moral principles, while others violate these moral principles. My informants gave me examples of God rewarding good people by healing them, and of punishing bad people by causing them to suffer illnesses. Similarly, success and failure in a material or social sense can be accounted for in terms of supernatural justice. Apparently, however, the primary instrumentality of supernatural justice is illness and healing. My informants insisted that all healing is through God's intervention. A doctor and modern medicine may be necessary in healing, but they are never sufficient. My informants pointed out to me cases in which people enjoyed the best available medical attention, but who died in spite of it. Furthermore, they told me stories about people with apparently incurable illnesses who were cured by God alone, through the persons of faith healers like Oral Roberts.

In contrast, fate is an eminently amoral principle. Bad people sometimes enjoy the best things in life while good people suffer misfortunes. Unlike supernatural justice, as an ethical or religious principle fate is not consistent with the basic nature of culture and society. It may, however, be interpreted as a divinized recognition of a fundamental disjunction that has recently been emphasized by Claude Lévi-Strauss; that is, although culture is somehow a part of nature, they are two realms which coincide imperfectly.[12] In other words, through culture, man is able to plan his affairs and expect good outcomes, but through the recalcitrance of nature, his plans often go awry. Thus, my informants told me a story about two farmers, both of whom were morally good and equally capable, who owned adjacent farms. But one of these farmers prospered while the other failed. Supernatural justice accounted for the prosperous farmer, but it could not account for the farmer who failed.

It should be obvious that my informants cannot be said to be fatalistic in the sense that fate determines everything that happens. Each person has a fate which is determined by God, but it is only a kind of outline map, with many spaces left blank. Properly speaking, even God does not know in advance everything a person will do, though he perhaps knows about it when it happens or after it happens. In other words, this concept of fate does not deny the existence of free will. In the words of my informant, "Each person makes his own life."

For example, my informants explained that each person has as a gift from God a "talent" or "calling" which determines the kind of work he does in life. The manner in which a person becomes aware of his calling is quite straightforward: he merely tries several jobs, and when he finds one that is agreeable, he knows what his calling is. What could be more effective than this? However, my informants told me of several cases in which people knew what their calling was, but tried to escape it. In one case a person who did this suffered supernatural punishment. Consistent with this, my informants felt that no one should attempt to influence another person's choice of career; the discovery of calling is purely an individual matter.

In addition to a calling, a person's fate includes a number of "blessings," "trials," and the time and manner of death. Blessings are the good things in life. They are given to good and bad people alike, and they are unevenly distributed. Some people get a lot, and others get little, but a person is not supposed to ponder about this, and he must under no circumstances make invidious comparisons between his own blessings and those of others. Trials are the bad things in life, such as illness and the death of loved ones. All people may expect trials and tribulations, even people who are good in the highest moral sense. "It rains on the just and the unjust alike." Finally, the time and manner of a person's death is fixed by God. To prove this, my informants gave me examples of horrible automobile wrecks in which no one was injured, and, on the contrary, of relatively minor wrecks in which someone died. Thus, an automobile wreck might be a material cause of death, but it is not a sufficient cause.[13] Likewise, people can choose to alter the time of their death by committing suicide. But this, like the avoidance of one's calling, is regarded as sinful.

Drawing the strands of this analysis together, we see that in the fundamentalist Christian belief-system meaningful events in life are explained in terms of two contradictory principles. However, I must emphasize here that contradictory is the judgment of an outside observer. My informants did not see any contradiction between supernatural justice and fate, and they would insist that no contradiction exists. That is, the contradiction between supernatural justice and fate is absorbed in the mysterious nature of God. God, for the most part, is just, but his nature is not wholly transparent. As my informants said, "God works in mysterious ways." Furthermore, it is not befitting that a man seek to penetrate this mystery too deeply. They told me, for example, about a man who tried to do this by studying the Bible with great application and intensity; eventually, and almost inevitably, he became mad. Thus, the part of God's nature that is known to man explains supernatural justice, but fate comes from a part of God's nature that is unknown to man, and it is moreover a part of God's nature that man should not attempt to know.

Thus, it is not correct to say that the nature of the fundamentalist Christian God is simply human nature in a divinized form. This opaque or obscure part of God's nature is particularly relevant to the third class of events recognized by the fundamentalist belief-system. According to my informants, these events are signs and warnings. They are events which are not of a magnitude to require explanation in terms of fate or supernatural justice, nor are they as trivial as events which can be accounted for in terms of accident, choice, or skill. They are precisely the events through which God communicates with man. The critical thing here, though, is that the correct interpretation of these events depends upon a person's having the right ritual condition. As we shall presently see, people who are not "saved" are unable to understand the meaning of these events. The only exception is that God gives warnings to unsaved people to the effect that they not defer salvation any longer.

Signs and warnings are alike in that they are events which indicate or foretell events in the future, but there is apparently a difference in magnitude in that warnings foretell events of more importance than are foretold by signs. The meaning of a sign, if apprehended before the fact, is usually ambiguous. For example, my informants said that when an owl hoots in one's back yard, it means that "somebody is going to die." The event is foretold, but the identity of the person who is to die is unknown. Often, these signs are recalled after the fact; after the event happens, a sign is recalled which, if it had been correctly interpreted, would have predicted the event.

Warnings foretell events of a more serious nature, and they furthermore often mean that God is about to inflict supernatural punishment. My informant told me the following story as an illustration of how God communicates with people.

As I drove up to the house in my car and saw the tree (that stood beside it), I thought about a woman who was killed by lightning. I hadn't thought about her for several years. I didn't park under the tree where I usually parked. As I was walking into the house, lightning struck the tree, and it was like somebody clapped his hands over my ears. It tore the tree all to pieces. I looked up and the sun was shining.

This was one of the most important events in my informant's life. It convinced him that it was time to be saved, and he subsequently was.

III

Up to this point, I have been almost exclusively concerned with structure in a logical, nontemporal sense. The task has been to analyze beliefs and their systematic interconnections with each other. I now undertake the second step in the analysis; the task now is to show in a preliminary way how this nontemporal structure fits into the structure of society, that is, into an event structure.

Because the connections between this belief-system and the social system in which it exists are manifold, the following analysis is highly incomplete. For example, the notion of "calling" clearly fits a society with considerable occupational specialization. Similarly, the notion of "blessings" and their somewhat erratic allocation clearly fits a society in which there are considerable differences in wealth. Also, if there are any functionalists still around, they will see that the function of the rule against invidious comparison is to support the existing socio-economic order.

However, the aspect of social life I wish to emphasize here pertains to the life cycle of the individual. We have seen that an individual is said to be born without a mind, and by implication, he is unable to communicate with or to understand God. In contrast, my informants insisted that the Devil is in children. They said that even small infants can "lie a little." For example, they sometimes cry when there is nothing wrong with them, just for the sake of getting attention. This does not mean that children are consequently evil, as has sometimes been assumed; it means that although the Devil is "in" children, they are not old enough to do anything really bad, but they are capable of "devilment."

As a person grows older, and as his mind develops, his relationship with God becomes more and more critical. At the same time, the Devil is thought to gain a stronger and stronger hold on a person's being. By the time a person is a young adult, this conflict is most intense. This is precisely the time when a person is expected to be saved, i.e., he is supposed to cast out the Devil and align himself with God.

"Salvation" is an extremely complicated social institution. In theory, it can happen to an individual at any time, at any place; in practice, it almost always takes the form of a rite of passage that occurs in church. One of my informants described the actual event in vivid psychological terms: he felt the presence of and conflict between God and the Devil; he felt that God was calling him to the altar while the hands of the Devil literally held him back; at the moment of salvation, he said the Devil was "thrown out"; and after salvation my informant said that he felt "light as a feather" and that "a great weight had been lifted" from him.

Thus, salvation is both a social and ideological pivot. Socially it means that before salvation a person is merely on the fringes of society, but after being saved he is wholly within society and is fully accountable. My informant insisted that one cannot fully trust a person who has not been saved. Ideologically, it means that a person after salvation has full access to the belief-system. As we have seen, a person who is not saved does not know how to interpret God's meaning; this amounts to saying that a person who is not saved does not understand life. In this sense, we may say that the belief-system consists of deep knowledge, while all other knowledge is shallow or simple. To this latter point, I will return later.

My informants did not claim that salvation solves all of a person's problems. He can still expect trials and tribulations, but even these will assume a new significance and meaning. Above all, salvation enables him to make some kind of sense out of the world in which he finds himself.

IV

In conclusion, I have attempted to show that the beliefs which make up this fundamentalist Christian belief-system fit neatly together in a coherent, even elegant system, such that one belief is not fully intelligible apart from the others. In this light, it becomes obvious that many of the generalizations that have been made about fundamentalist Christians in general, and about working-class Christians in particular, make very little sense. For example, that they believe that man is inherently evil at birth, that they believe in a capricious God, that they believe in a wholly just God, and especially that they are fatalistic. If my analysis is correct, fatalism and free will are complementary, and may in fact be found to stand in this relationship to each other in other belief-systems. The critical question is what is the extent to which an individual is held socially responsible for what he does. In answer to this, I am rather sure that my working-class informants hold an individual responsible to a far greater degree than many middle-class people of a Freudian persuasion.[14]

I have approached this material structurally, attempting to reveal the ideational structures which lie behind outward expressions of thought. Thus, the elemental agencies of God, the mind, and the Devil constitute a basic structural pattern. As we have seen, subsidiary beliefs such as "speaking in unknown tongues" can easily be fitted into this pattern, and, structurally speaking, the addition makes far less difference than is commonly believed. This does not, of course, mean that this "slight" difference is unimportant to believers as a means of distinguishing themselves from other sects or churches.

Although the attempt to penetrate expressed thought in order to discern underlying structures is hazardous from the standpoint of methodology, we are not likely to make much progress in the comparative study of belief-systems until we are able to do this.[15] Some ethnographic information suggests that we are justified in searching out underlying structures of thought. The Dogon of the French Sudan, for example, explicitly distinguish between "deep knowledge" and "simple knowledge," saying that "simple knowledge . . . is . . . only a beginning in the understanding of beliefs and customs." [16]

Even this present modest and admittedly preliminary analysis of fundamentalist Christian beliefs suggests some rather interesting structural comparisons. For example, the structural alignment and interrelationships among God, the mind, and the Devil are strikingly similar to the structural alignment and interrelationships among the Freudian superego, ego, and id. This structural parallelism or congruity is not surprising when we recall the enthusiastic rapidity with which middle-class Christians accepted the popular version of Freudian theory.[17] Thus it seems that they simply plugged Freudian concepts and principles into a preexisting structural pattern. Freud's theory was different, but it could not be too different, else intellectual assimilation would have been too difficult.

Other lines of comparative inquiry are suggested by my analysis of the role of contradiction in the fundamentalist Christian belief-system. In his analysis of the Kalabari world view, Robin Horton has shown how contradictions which are inherent in one level of thought and experience (e.g., everyday life) are explained by spiritual beings (e.g., God) which are postulated to exist at higher levels of experience and thought, and these beings are moreover believed to have extraordinary properties. Thus, through a structural necessity, shall we say, deities are only partially personalized or anthropomorphic. And as Horton points out, hierarchies of theoretical models are postulated in the natural sciences in a manner quite similar to the hierarchies in systems of traditional thought.[18]

I think it can be argued that basic contradictions are probably present in all traditional systems of thought. Arising from the nature of the human condition, these contradictions are largely responsible for the closed nature of traditional thought. A belief-system is able to account for many events because it contains contradictory principles. The system, in fact, becomes exceptionless. Supernatural justice, in some sense, affirms that society and culture are well formed, while fate, in some sense, affirms that they are basically imperfect. Anthropologists have found it useful to define religion as the extension of beliefs and norms governing social relationships into the realm of deities and personalized agencies.[19] This is equivalent to saying that in all systems of traditional thought we should find the principle of supernatural justice, as I have used the term. I would like to propose that all such systems of belief in addition contain an amoral principle, such as witchcraft, fate, or the unconscious self.[20] With this conceptual equipment, a belief-system can explain everything that requires explanation.

In closing, I must point out certain limitations on the substance of this research. First, at the time I did this research, I was largely unaware of the theories and concepts I have subsequently used in my analysis. Although this suggests that my selection of facts was not biased by my theory and also that the theories are in fact useful, if I were to do the research today I would ask many additional questions. In particular, perhaps as a consequence of my failure to adequately discuss death with my informants, I have virtually no information on their notion of the soul, nor of the relationship between soul and mind. Thus, my information is somewhat incomplete. Second, because of a total reliance on participant observation, I do not know the social distribution of this belief-system. For example, in what sense does it hold for, say, middle-class whites or low-income blacks? I would suspect that the basic structure of the belief-system would hold for middle-class whites, though with certain differences in the subsidiary beliefs. I also suspect that some basic divergences might be found in the beliefs of low-income southern black people, some of whom retain a belief in witchcraft. But these are only guesses.

NOTES

1. Samuel S. Hill, Jr., *Southern Churches in Crisis* (New York: Holt, Rinehart & Winston, 1966), pp. 99-102; "Research in Religion," in *Perspectives on the South: Agenda for Research*, Edgar T. Thompson, ed. (Durham, N. C.: Duke University Press, 1967), pp. 195-213. See chap. 1, above.

2. I first wrote up this data as a master's thesis and later presented portions of it in a paper at the 1967 meeting of the Society for the Scientific Study of Religion. I cannot possibly mention everyone who has read this paper, but I am particularly grateful to Frederick L. Bates, David Hargrove, H. Eugene Hodges, John J. Honigmann, Richard Lieban, James L. Peacock, Richard Simpson, and Donald

South, who read this paper in various stages of preparation, giving me benefit of their criticism.

3. Jack Goody and Ian Watt, "The Consequences of Literacy," *Comparative Studies in Society and History*, V (1962-1963), 304-45.

4. Cf. Robin Horton, "The Kalabari World-View: An Outline and Interpretation," *Africa*, XXXII (July, 1962) 197-220; "African Traditional Thought and Western Science," *Africa*, XXXVII (1967), 50-71, 155-87.

5. Meyer Fortes, *Oedipus and Job in West African Religion* (Cambridge: Cambridge University Press, 1959). The adjectival form of "Tallensi" is "Tale."

6. Robin Horton has criticized Fortes on two grounds. First, the fate that tragically governed Oedipus' life was not a part of his personality, while the Tale notion of bad destiny is clearly a part of the individual's personality. And second, in classical Greek thought fate or destiny cannot be modified, while Tale bad destiny can sometimes be modified or exorcised entirely. Horton argues that Fortes should have dispensed with the Greek notion of fate and used instead the Freudian notion of an unconscious self, which Horton demonstrates to be a far more exact parallel to Tale thinking. See Horton, "Destiny and the Unconscious in West Africa," *Africa*, XXXI (1961), 110-16.

7. Lucien Lévy-Bruhl was the first to notice the prevalence of contradiction in nonwestern belief-systems, making it one of the defining characteristics of "preliterate mentality." However, he did not explain its function or significance.

8. In studies of belief-systems is it essential that we clearly distinguish between autochthonous and analytical concepts. I have here adopted the convention of putting the first occurrence of analytical concepts in italics and the first occurrence of autochthonous concepts in quotes. Previously introduced, both *fate* and *supernatural justice* are analytical concepts.

9. I did not press my informants on this point, I suspect, however, that if it does turn out that communication with the Devil is possible, it will be judged to be extraordinary, deviant, or antisocial.

10. I have had to rely on analytical concepts rather heavily in this structural analysis. It seems that in every belief-system some of the concepts and principles, often the more important ones, are implicit and hence rather inaccessible to ordinary thought. Moreover, if a further defense of analytical concepts is necessary, I would argue that they do not detract from my analysis any more than the linguists' use of analytical concepts such as *phoneme, morpheme, noun class*, and so on in their structural analyses of languages.

   As a further methodological precaution, a number of southern Protestant ministers and laymen have read through this analysis, and they have assented to its general accuracy. On this methodological rule, cf. John Beattie, *Other Cultures* (New York: Free Press of Glencoe, 1964), pp. 65-77; D. F. Pocock, *Social Anthropology* (London: Sheed and Ward, 1961), pp. 83-90.

11. This comes out very clearly in Tom Wolfe's "Last American Hero," a biographical essay about Junior Johnson, a stockcar racer who for many good old boys is an almost mythical figure. See *The Kandy-Kolored Tangerine-Flake Streamline Baby* (New York: Farrar, Straus & Giroux, 1963), pp. 127-72.

12. Claude Lévi-Strauss, *Totemism* (Boston: Beacon Press, 1962); *The Savage Mind* (Chicago: University of Chicago Press, 1966).

13. My informants frequently illustrated their belief-system by telling stories involving automobiles, thus confirming the accuracy of the observations in Tom Wolfe's essay cited *supra*. Incidentally, this explanation of death would make sense to the Azande, who say of witchcraft that it is *umbaga*, or the second spear. "Hence if a man is killed by an elephant Azande say that the elephant is the first

141

spear and that witchcraft is the second spear and that together they killed the man." E. E. Evans-Pritchard, *Witchcraft, Oracles and Magic among the Azande* (Oxford: Clarendon Press, 1937), p. 74.

14. Cf. Horton, "Destiny and the Unconscious," pp. 115-16.

15. Calling it "empirical philosophy," Rodney Needham has recently written that the comparative study of belief-systems is the distinctive task of social anthropology. See his review of G. E. R. Lloyd's *Polarity and Analogy* in the *American Anthropologist*, LXIX (June-August, 1967), 384-85.

16. G. Dieterlen, Introduction to *Conversations with Ogotemmeli*, by Marcel Griaule (London: Oxford University Press, 1965), pp. xiv-xv.

17. Cf. Horton, "Destiny and the Unconscious."

18. Horton, "Kalabari World-View."

19. Horton, "A Definition of Religion and Its Uses," *Royal Anthropological Institute Journal*, XC (1960), 201-26.

20. Fortes, *Oedipus*, observes that fate and witchcraft explain the same sorts of events; Horton, "Destiny and the Unconscious," makes the same observation for fate and the unconscious self. Thus, witchcraft, fate, and the unconscious self are structurally equivalent.

6
RELIGIOUS DEMOGRAPHY OF THE SOUTH

While demography shows signs of significant new application these days, the demographic and geographic study of religion is as yet barely off the ground. What I have to say here will be so couched in generalities, so hedged by uncertainties, as to cause any genuine demographer considerable alarm and no doubt some unsettling dismay. Detailed local studies that are reliable and current will be conspicuous by their absence. But overviews can do two things at least: (1) give some notion of trends and patterns; and (2) give some direction for further investigations.

It is the case that atlas makers and census takers have lost rather than seized opportunities for analytic treatment of religion. This is generally true worldwide as well as in the United States. To restrict ourselves to the latter area, we may note that American maps and atlases on deposit with the Library of Congress rarely focus on religion.

"In the older work of Philip Lee Phillips, *A List of Works Relating to Cartography* (Washington: Government Printing Office, 1901), no map listed has religion as its major concern, though the location of churches is incidentally indicated on some. From 1953 to 1955, when the Library published an annual catalogue of maps received, the only item of ecclesiastical cartography noted was a diocesan map of the Roman Catholic Church in the United States (Bruce Publishing Company). Recent historical atlases have, for the most part, little to offer. James Truslow Adams' *Atlas of American History* (New York: C. Scribner's Sons, 1943) contains no example of ecclesiastical mapping, while Clifford Lee and Elizabeth H. Lord's *Historical Atlas of the United States* (New York: H. Holt and Company, 1944; rev. ed., 1953) covers wars, crops, courts, colleges, fisheries, and the average temperature in July—but not religion. (Map 280 does show the dry counties in America in 1942; the opportunity, however, to present a comparable map of religious distribution is not seized. But see Andrew Sinclair, *Prohibition: The Era of Excess* [Boston: Little, Brown, 1962], pp. 66-67.)

"From the perspective of religion, geographies of America got off to a rather good start with Jedidiah Morse's *The American Geography*, first published in Elizabeth Town (New Jersey) in 1789; a second edition appeared in London in 1792, and many editions followed in the succeeding decades. Although Morse's careful attention to religion is probably due more to his clerical status than to an intense concern about the interrelation of religion and geography, his work would be destined, one might suppose, to have a powerful influence on subsequent American geographers. Such, however, is not the case. Albert Perry Brigham's *Geographic Influences in American History* (Boston: Ginn and Company, 1903) contains neither sentence nor sketch pertaining to religion. And the same is true of Ralph Hall Brown's more recent *Historical Geography of the United States* (New York: Harcourt, Brace, 1948), except for its brief mention of Catholic missions and Mormon colonies." [1]

Four works have made more systematic stabs in the direction of pattern plotting for American religion. The well-known older work of Charles O. Paullin and John K. Wright, *Atlas of the Historical Geography of the United States* (published in 1932 jointly by the Carnegie Institute in Washington and the American Geographical Society in New York) shows the location of churches in three periods of American history: 1775, 1860, and 1890. In the mid 1950s, the Bureau of Research and Survey of the National Council of Churches issued a series of eighty bulletins under the general title *Churches and Church Membership in the United States* (New York, 1956-58). These bulletins presented the first county-by-county data for the nation since the federal government abandoned the gathering of religious statistics in 1936. Utilizing these data, Wilbur Zelinsky of Southern Illinois University presented suggestive maps in a major article entitled "An Approach to the Religious Geography of the United States: Patterns of Church Membership in 1952" (*Annals of the Association of American Geographers*, LI [June, 1961]). And in 1962 the present writer published an *Historical Atlas of Religion in America* (New York: Harper & Row).

All four of these survey efforts have severe limitations, but it will be easiest to speak of those in my own work. This can be done in most relevant fashion by turning to the title of a recent conference, "The Bible Belt in Continuity and Change." Now Bible Belt is one geographical term that does have the sanction of common usage. It also, unfortunately, has the maddening elusiveness of popular phrases. Just where and just what is the Bible Belt? You may turn in confident expectation to my *Atlas* for an answer: sadly, you will not find it there. For the necessary geographical refinement—to say nothing of the required theological refinement—has not been made. For example, to draw the Bible Belt meaningfully would probably require that we pay a good deal of attention to relief lines of a map, to the mountains and valleys, the gaps and passes, the arable or inhospitable lands. We might also need to examine the role of urbanization in cinching or loosening that belt. A dozen questions about ethnic and denominational backgrounds, about migration and industrialization patterns, about education and occupation have to be answered before the cartographer can—with any real justification—draw, label, or color a Bible Belt.

So the question, "What and where is the Bible Belt?" will not receive a full answer here either. What I would propose are some of the kinds of data that can help define religion in the South. And whether we wish to cling to or discard our familiar if vague metaphor is another (and postponable) question. First, some general characteristics. Nationally, the major religious families are ranked in this numerical order:

	Membership in millions (1965)
1. Roman Catholic	46.2
2. Baptist	23.6
3. Methodist	14.3
4. Lutheran	8.8
5. Presbyterian	4.4

Regionally, that is in the South (defined to include these states: Maryland, West Virginia, Virginia, North Carolina, Tennessee, Kentucky, South Carolina, Georgia, Florida, Alabama, Mississippi, Louisiana, Arkansas, and Texas), the ranking would be as follows:

	Membership in the South (1965)
1. Baptist	13.4
2. Methodist	4.3
3. Christian and Churches of Christ	3.0
4. Presbyterian	1.0
5. Episcopalian	.8

Roman Catholics and Lutherans are the conspicuous dropouts as we shift from the national to the southern scene, while the Christian and Episcopal fellowships move up in rank.

Another way to emphasize regional peculiarities is provided by a Gallup sampling in 1967. The following list indicates the percentage of each religious body's membership within the South: [2]

Baptist	57%
Methodist	30%
Episcopal	25%
Presbyterian	23%
Roman Catholic	9%
Lutheran	8%
Jewish	3%

Gallup had no figures on Disciples of Christ or Churches of Christ.

Percentages and rankings have their limits, too, in providing a mental image of religion in the South. Thus it would be well to examine distribution patterns for religion throughout the South. This will be done on the basis of a county-by-county analysis of the strength of the churches. Verbally this would take an intolerable amount of time, but visually it can be accomplished with some dispatch. Patterns of growth between the nineteenth and twentieth centuries and among the major denominations will be compared—where the data will permit.

A. THE EPISCOPAL CHURCHES

The Church of England, more than any other ecclesiastical group, had a head start in the South. And its planting there was firmer than in any other section of early America. The mother country raised funds, the colonial assemblies passed laws, and royal governors smiled with favor on the establishment of England's church in the colonial South. The chances for monopolistic dominance looked very good, but this promise, as we know, was never fulfilled.

Yet, after national independence, the newly created Protestant Episcopal Church maintained a steady base in the South, especially in those tidewater regions where its initial establishment was most secure. On the 1850 map, Maryland's and South Carolina's coastal regions are more impressively Episcopal than are Virginia's. North Carolina and Georgia show even less penetration, of course, but this accurately reflects the earlier weakness of Anglicanism in those two areas. In South Carolina, the obvious strength of the Episcopal Church in Beaufort and Charleston counties spills over in only slightly diminished fashion into Colleton, Orangeburg, and Clarendon. The Florida impact is chiefly a missionary one. Curiously, Alabama's Anglicanism appears stronger than Georgia's, but the latter is only more scattered. There were twenty churches in Georgia in 1850, seventeen in Alabama.

In 1950, the original colonies—with the exception of Georgia—continue to show significant Episcopal strength. Florida has come into the picture prominently, but the artificial, migratory character of Florida's population will always make that area a special case. Like Washington, D. C., and its immediate environs, observations concerning Florida will not tell us much about religion in the South. By 1950 Alabama has overtaken Georgia in the number of Episcopal churches (99 to 87), and I do not have any ready explanation for this. On both sides of the Mississippi River and in East Texas, the coverage is of above average density.

We are not yet talking about the giant powers of southern religion, of course, but clearly the Episcopal Church is a pervasive, stable, and significant element in that ethos.

B. ROMAN CATHOLIC CHURCHES

Because England's Catholicism, like England's Anglicanism, is also involved in the settling of a southern colony, namely, Maryland, it is appropriate to consider its stability or pervasiveness in the South. Colonial Maryland had many problems religiously, and Catholicism took quite a beating on its own ground. Nevertheless, as the 1850 map reveals, Maryland continued to be a principal base, indeed the principal base for English-speaking Catholicism. Elsewhere in the South, however, Catholicism shows little evidence of a strong colonial stamp except for France's Louisiana. With the founding of Mobile in 1702 and New Orleans in 1718, French Catholicism gained a foothold never lost.

In the mid-twentieth century, the picture of Catholicism in the South is not radically altered. Maryland and southern Louisiana outdistance all the rest. Louisiana, for example, has more Catholic churches (365) than do Virginia (92), North Carolina (125), South Carolina (76), and Georgia (40) combined. In eastern and southern Texas, the Spanish phase of American history is graphically evident—much more so than in Florida, for example, where the contemporary Catholicism is not Spanish despite Spain's heroic and costly efforts in earlier time. Thus on the whole Catholicism is on the fringes, so to speak, of southern culture: the fringes of Maryland to the north, Florida to the south, Louisiana and segments of Texas to the west.

C. BAPTIST CHURCHES

In early America the Baptist centers of strength were not in the South. In Rhode Island and in and around Philadelphia, the denomination had its power bases—though "power" is really too strong a word for this colonial group. In the middle of the eighteenth century, for example, only twenty-five Baptist churches were to be found in all of the South, and over one half of these were in North Carolina.

That Baptists were latecomers to southern culture is evident, I think, from the 1850 map. Note the sparseness of Baptist settlement in the tidewater regions—all the way from Delaware to the Gulf shores of Florida, Alabama, Mississippi, and Louisiana. Unlike Methodists, the Baptists did not expand through the instrument of circuit riding but of local, settled preaching. And the farmer-preachers had to go where land was still available, still relatively cheap. After the Great Awakening clergy migrating down from New England and the Middle Colonies were also looking for areas where tradition, laws, and "churchmen" all were fewer.

If one might be inclined to identify Baptists with "Bible-Beltness," then it should be noted that the Belt is a development of the interior: the upper reaches of the Savannah River, the more mountainous areas of North Carolina, Tennessee, and Kentucky, the more remote regions of Alabama and Mississippi. The Blue Ridge Mountains, on the other hand, already had significant Germanic settlements by the time Baptists came in sizable number. That region was rather inhospitable in 1850 and remained so a century later.

In 1950 Baptists in the South are still concentrated more in the interior regions. Maryland, most of Virginia, and eastern North Carolina are surprisingly light for a century characterized by major population shifts. The epicenter for Baptists would not be Atlanta or Richmond or Charleston but somewhere around Maryville or Knoxville, Tennessee.

Now Negro Baptists raise special problems whose solutions can only be suggested. These data reflected on the map do not include Negro Baptists because comparable statistics were unavailable. There are seven or eight million Negro Baptist in the entire country, however, so it makes no sense to ignore this glaring weakness in our data. About sixty-three percent of Negro Christians are Baptists, another twenty-three percent Methodist. Together this represents almost four-fifths of American Negroes with a church affiliation. The few detailed studies that have been done in urban areas indicate a severe challenge to this supremacy.

This challenge comes not only in the form of a general secularism (either apathetic or militant) but also in the form of the Black Muslims and a variety of ecstatic, charismatic sectarian movements.[3]

D. METHODIST CHURCHES

Since Methodism is a late arrival on the total American scene—not just the southern scene, one might expect it to be largely excluded from the easternmost areas. Except for the indomitable circuit rider this might well have been true. That, however, is an all-important exception. Thus Cape Cod, Long Island, Delaware, and the Eastern Shore of Maryland quickly became and long remained major Methodist centers. From these points, as the 1850 map shows, Methodism tended to move more in a westerly than in a southerly direction. It followed the post roads and opened up the frontiers. Except for the strength around Charleston, South Carolina, the Deep South is relatively weak in comparison with the old Northwest.

In the present century the westward bent of Methodism is even more apparent, looking now only at the South. It is *West* Virginia, *western* North Carolina, *western* Tennessee, and *western* Alabama that most clearly bear a Methodist mark. Along the Atlantic coast, Maryland and South Carolina continue to be very strong, most notably the former. However, both Ohio and Pennsylvania have more Methodist churches than does any southern state— except Texas. This is not true, one hastens to add, of the companion southern giant: the Baptists. North Carolina has over three thousand Baptist churches within its borders, outranked nowhere in the North and only by Texas in the nation.

E. PRESBYTERIAN CHURCHES

Not until the eighteenth century was a presbytery of Scotch-Irish Presbyterians formed in America. Within fifty years of its formation, about two hundred thousand Scots, chiefly from Ulster, arrived in the colonies. Debarking generally at Philadelphia, they moved into western Pennsylvania, and then along valleys and rivers to the south or farther west.

In the 1850 map the centrality of western Pennsylvania in Presbyterian life hardly requires comment.[4] In its westward movement, Presbyterianism joined with Congregationalism in an 1801 plan of union for a common westward trek. In pressing all the way to the Pacific, "Presbygationists" dropped an impressive number of colleges en route and carried aspects of New England–Middle Colony Calvinism far beyond its native climes. In its southward conquests, Presbyterianism moved more on its own so that "southern Presbyterianism" was a distinct entity long before Civil War crises aggravated differences among the nation's Presbyterians.

The 1950 map shows the direction of southern migration to be largely southwesterly. One can almost fancy a line from Lancaster County drawn at 240° intersecting the major Presbyterian concentrations. This is too simple, of course, but it does lead us, among other places, to Cumberland country in Tennessee. And there a major schism lasting from 1810 to 1906 gave a further special flavor to Presbyterianism in the South. While Presbyterians do pervade the southern states, only rarely are they the dominant force. They do dominate in Hoke County, North Carolina, for example, and in the contiguous county appropriately named Scotland. (Names like Aberdeen and Bonnie Doone also dot this area.) A little farther to the west, Mecklenburg County likewise contains more Presbyterians than it does the members of any other denominational group. In Virginia, Bath and Rockbridge counties continue to reflect, even to the present day, the strength of the eighteenth century migrations down from Pennsylvania.

A final comment about Presbyterianism in the South may

help explain its failure to become a more dominant force in this region. Southern Presbyterians, unlike Southern Baptists, remained in a minority status within their own denominational family. While Southern Baptists grew to six or eight times the size of their northern counterpart, Southern Presbyterians from 1861 to 1961 have continued to be only one-fourth the size of the parent. Again, by contrast with the Southern Baptist Convention, the Presbyterian Church, U.S., has been confined geographically to the limits—roughly—of the old Confederacy.

F. CONGREGATIONAL CHURCHES

Comment on the growth of Congregationalism in the South need not be extensive since the growth itself was not. It is appropriate, however, to consider this movement here, for Congregationalists and Presbyterians were allied —as previously noted—in their westward movement. Moving west from its strong base in New England would not normally lead Congregationalism in the direction of the southern states. In a sense the Middle Colony base of Presbyterianism served as a buffer to keep Congregationalists from achieving great southern strength.

The 1850 map shows the geographical particularity of Congregationalism in America. It also shows the primary direction in which the "New England mind" moved. Puritans in Dorchester, Massachusetts, sent a congregation to South Carolina in 1692 where, promptly, a new Dorchester came into being. A half-century later, a group of these South Carolina Congregationalists migrated due west to Midway (Liberty), Georgia, to establish that colony's only Congregational church (and to establish, thereby, an important center of patriot activity in the Revolutionary period). An even earlier penetration into Nansemond County, Virginia, had faded from view by the mid-nineteenth century, but has reasserted itself in the twentieth century.

In the 1950 map, the essential westward drive is even more evident. The increased representation in the South reveals the conscious efforts of Congregationalism to break out of the ethnic and geographical mold, especially by specific overtures to two groups: the freed Negro and the immigrant German. In North Carolina, notably in Alamance, Randolph, and Wake counties, Congregationalism is particularly strong. The county in Alabama with greatest congregational strength is also a Randolph. Both Elon College in Alamance County, North Carolina, and a junior college in Randolph County, Alabama, stem from the schism led by James O'Kelly in Virginia. In 1794 the "Christian Church" was founded in Virginia and in 1931 this "General Connection" merged with Congregationalism. Thus migration patterns from North Carolina may be presumed, though additional data are called for to show the nature and extent of the move. A few miles to the west of Randolph County lies Talladega, Alabama, a major center of Congregational educational effort among the Negroes. It is a likely guess—but at the moment only that—that the string of Congregational churches in Alabama north and south of Talladega grew from the educational-ecclesiastical labors of Northern Congregationalists in the era of Reconstruction. The same may be said of the Atlanta area where in 1865 Congregationalists led in the formation of Atlanta University, and to a lesser extent of Tougaloo, Mississippi, where four years later (1869) a similar venture was launched. The strength in Florida stems, of course, from modern migrations out of the Northeast, while that in tidewater Virginia harks back to the days when Governor William Berkeley did his best to drive the pesky Puritans out of his jurisdiction. With the possible exception of Virginia and North Carolina, Congregationalism nonetheless remains a religion of modest proportion in the South. For a surprisingly large number of Southerners, it remains a religion wholly unknown.

G. CHURCHES OF THE CAMPBELLITE MOVEMENT

Native to America, the denominations arising from the labors of Alexander Campbell and Barton Stone hold special interest for the region we are examining. Not until the 1830s does the movement have sufficient unity to enable us to follow its course even in a rough fashion. But county-by-county analysis is not possible for that period, nor for many decades later.

In mid-nineteenth century, Alexander Campbell himself offered an estimate of the size and distribution of the Disciples of Christ. About three-fourths of the fellowship were in six states: Ohio, Indiana, Illinois, Missouri, Kentucky, and Tennessee. The 1950 map shows these states—with one exception—still to be the principal areas. The one exception is Tennessee, and something has happened there which we shall come to shortly. Staying with the Disciples map a moment longer, we note a spread in the South that is from west to east—unlike all others we have so far considered. From West Virginia and nothern Kentucky, Disciples have moved eastward—or the path of conversions has moved eastward—into Virginia and eastern North Carolina. The Deep South, however, is without major penetration by the Disciples.

What happened in Tennessee brings us to the other half of the story: the Church of Christ schism from the parent body. Rejecting national conventions or societies, Sunday schools, settled pastors, and above all "mechanical music," the Churches of Christ assume the status of a separate denomination by the beginning of the present century. It is this group which has dominated Tennessee along with Texas to the disadvantage of the Disciples of Christ.

In a 1960 map the potency of this brotherhood in Tennessee is unmistakable. From Tennessee across Arkansas and Oklahoma into Texas is a real belt—perhaps more a Bible belt (or "Bible crescent") than any other region can offer. Contrary to popular assumption, the Churches of Christ are not primarily a phenomenon of the Deep South but of the border states. The strength in Alabama is clearly a spill over from Tennessee rather than an indigenous movement. Any analysis of religion in the South must surely reckon with the Churches of Christ, but clearly it is important to know with *which* South, geographically, one is dealing.

H. QUAKER MEETINGS

Quakerism entered the South quite early, but it kept on the move. Outside of Rhode Island and Pennsylvania, it was characteristic—and prudent—of colonial Quakers to keep on the move. The Quakers had North Carolina virtually to themselves, however, for the last quarter of the seventeenth century. In this less than splendid isolation, Quakers did make major inroads, never wholly erased, in the center of the state.

The 1850 map shows Guilford, Randolph, Chatham, and Johnston counties with at least three meetings apiece. North Carolina's Quarterly Meeting was started as early as 1689. Maryland and the northernmost parts of Virginia also benefitted from the proximity of the great concentrations in Pennsylvania and New Jersey. Other than that, however, the South in 1850 is virtually devoid of organized Quaker activity. North Carolina was the only southern colony in which Quakers had sufficient strength and persistence to harass and eventually influence the government under which they lived.

Internal division and discord along with Quakerism's strong antislavery stand prevented any appreciable growth in the South in the ensuing one hundred years. The 1950 map is almost interchangeable with the 1850 one. Some movement into east Tennessee may be noted, but elsewhere in our region Quakerism's Inner Light burns feebly, if at all. Of course, Quaker Meetings did not grow in great numbers anywhere from 1850 to 1950, but significant western conquests were made in Ohio and Indiana at a time when slavery made southern areas peculiarly inhospitable. In 1950 North Carolina had more Quaker meetings (seventy-six) than all other southern and border states combined.

I. LUTHERAN CHURCHES

The great centers of Lutheranism in America are not in the South. Yet there have been significant southern enclaves from the eighteenth century to the present. And taking the word enclave somewhat more literally, with Lutheranism we introduce the first non-English-speaking group into the South. The seventeenth century Swedish settlements in Delaware had no perceptible influence in the South, but the eighteenth century Germanic migrations into Pennsylvania did affect the South.

The 1850 map delineates clearly the southwesterly migration out of Pennsylvania into the Shenandoah Valley and along nearby ridges. The pockets of Lutheranism in South and North Carolina also stand out, these being augmented by direct debarkation in the South, either at Charleston or Savannah. In South Carolina the first Lutheran Church was organized in 1735 in Orangeburg, and this remains a Lutheran center. Indeed, in the nearby counties of Lexington and Newberry, South Carolina, the strongest denomination today is Lutheran. North Carolina, which was fed both from Pennsylvania to the North and Charleston-Savannah to the South, built up lasting Lutheran communities most conspicuously in Rowan and Catawba counties.

By 1950 the changes in the South are relatively few except for the migrations into east and south Texas. There, surrounded by Catholics to the South and Baptists to the North, German Lutheran and Scandinavian Lutheran enclaves have persisted to the present (notably in Lee, Lavaca, and Gillespie counties). Elsewhere, the pattern is hardly altered. South and North Carolina along with the ridges of western Virginia account for most all of the remaining Lutherans in the South. (In 1950 Georgia, Alabama, Mississippi, and Louisiana had a total of 125 Lutheran Churches of all synods; Pennsylvania had 1,644.)

J. OTHER GROUPS, BRIEFLY NOTED

The German Reformed (later to become the Evangelical and Reformed and still later to be joined with Congregationalists in the United Church of Christ) penetrated the Appalachian Valley and western North Carolina in the eighteenth century. Neither by 1850 nor by 1950 is much further penetration evident. The Ohio River seems to serve almost as an inviolable border.

The Dutch Reformed has been a closely knit group from the seventeenth century to the present, as the 1850 and 1950 maps indicate. The relevance of this denomination to southern religion will be enhanced, however, should the proposed merger with the Presbyterian Church, U.S., be consummated.

Mormonism remains a phenomenon of the West despite its origin in upstate New York. The Reorganized Church of Jesus Christ, much smaller than the Utah Church, shows more promise of overcoming its geographical particularity than does the larger body. Neither church, however, is at present a major feature on the southern landscape.

Jewish population in America is heavily urban. So it is also in the South as Richmond, Atlanta, Birmingham, Memphis, Dallas, Houston, and Miami appear as obvious centers. But in total numbers, Jewish population in the South is sparse (three percent as previously noted). Only Florida ranks among the top ten states in percentage of citizens who are Jewish, and it is number ten with 2.27% as compared with New York's 14.06% or New Jersey's 5.27%. In the scattered communities across the South, the kind of Judaism most often encountered is Conservative rather than Orthodox or Reform. The most useful analyses of Judaism in the South will doubtless come by way of urban sociology, with attention paid primarily not to Jewish *population* but to Jewish *participation* in synagogue or temple activity.

This paper began with an indication that more reliable, current, local data are needed before we can really know when and where and what the Bible Belt really is. It closes on the same note, with the only half-facetious suggestion that somebody survey the major Bible publishers to see if the South, even on Marxian terms, really deserves the name!

NOTES

1. E. S. Gaustad, "Ecclesiastical Cartography in America," in *The Teacher's Yoke* (Waco: Baylor University Press, 1964), pp. 260-61.

2. *Gallup Opinion Index: Special Report on Religion 1967*, Princeton, New Jersey, pp. 15-23.

3. See Herbert W. Schneider, *Religion in 20th Century America*, rev. ed. (New York: Atheneum, 1964), Appendix A.

4. That lively region deserves a treatment comparable to Whitney R. Cross's *The Burned-over District* (Ithaca: Cornell University Press, 1950), which provides an excellent analysis of upstate New York.

EPISCOPAL CHURCHES: 1850

Number of churches per county

0   1-2   3-5   6-10   Over 10

Copyright © 1962 by Edwin Scott Gaustad

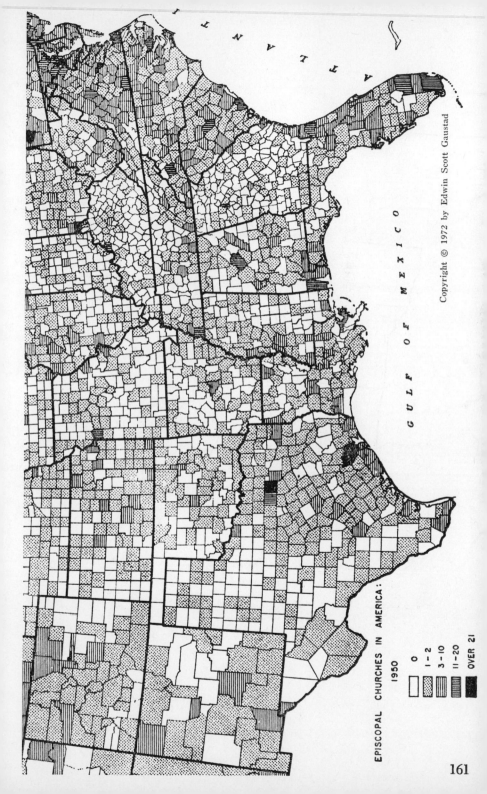

EPISCOPAL CHURCHES IN AMERICA:
1950

☐	0
▨	1 – 2
▧	3 – 10
▥	11 – 20
■	OVER 21

GULF OF MEXICO

ATLANTIC

ROMAN CATHOLIC CHURCHES: 1850

Number of churches per county

☐ 0 ▨ 1-2 ▨ 3-5 ▨ 6-10 ■ Over 10

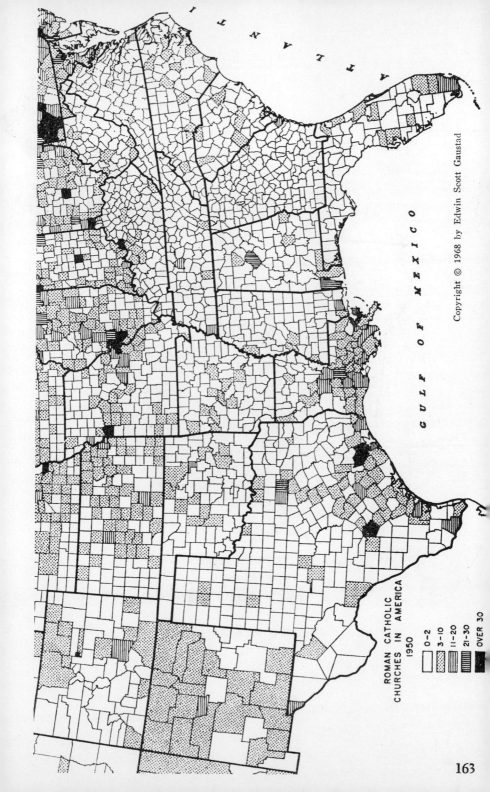

ROMAN CATHOLIC
CHURCHES IN AMERICA
1950

0–2
3–10
11–20
21–30
OVER 30

GULF OF MEXICO

ATLANTIC

Copyright © 1968 by Edwin Scott Gaustad

163

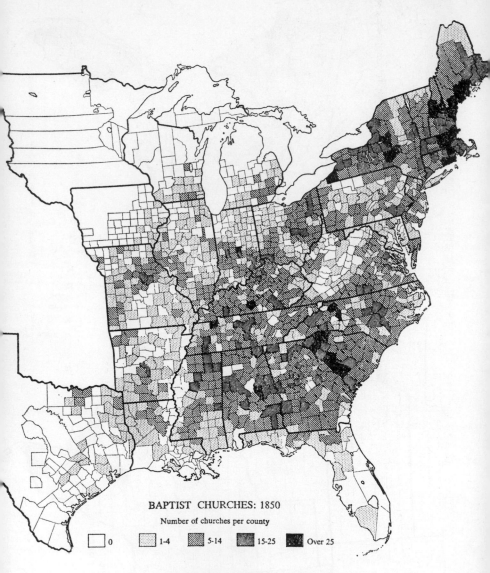

BAPTIST CHURCHES: 1850

Number of churches per county

0   1-4   5-14   15-25   Over 25

Copyright © 1962 by Edwin Scott Gaustad

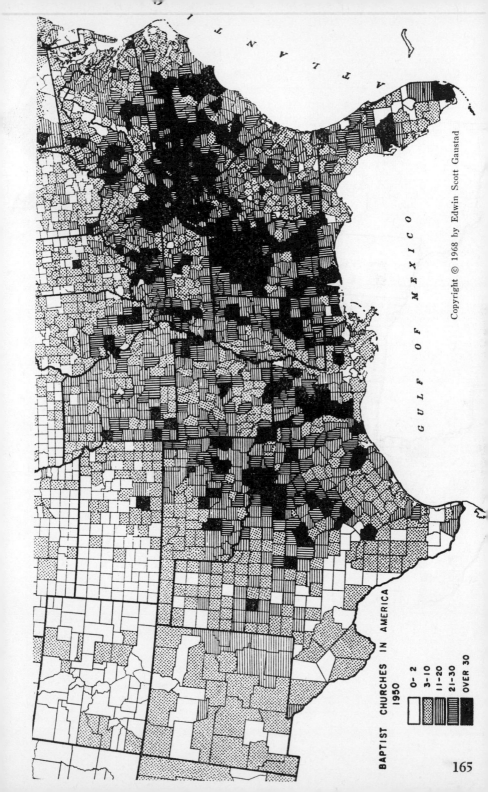

BAPTIST CHURCHES IN AMERICA
1950

0- 2
3-10
11-20
21-30
OVER 30

Copyright © 1968 by Edwin Scott Gaustad

165

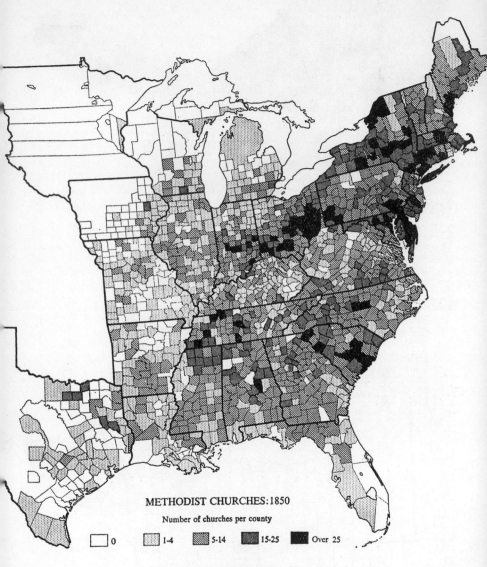

METHODIST CHURCHES: 1850

Number of churches per county

☐ 0   ▨ 1-4   ▨ 5-14   ▨ 15-25   ■ Over 25

Copyright © 1962 by Edwin Scott Gaustad

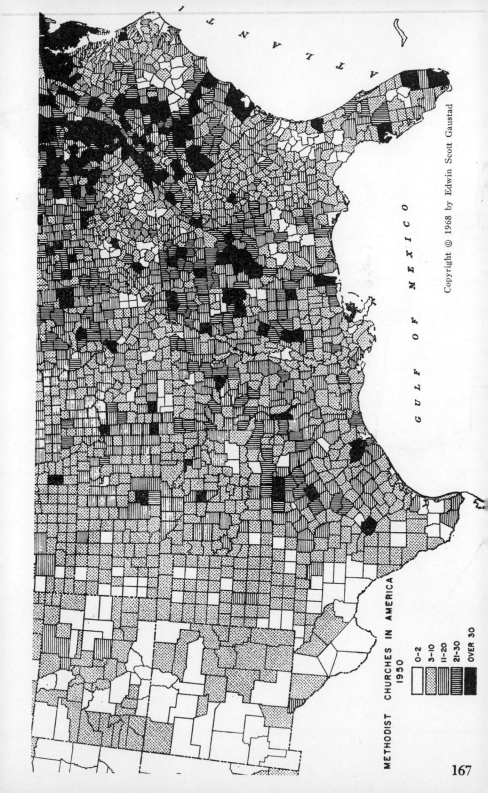

METHODIST CHURCHES IN AMERICA
1950

0-2
3-10
11-20
21-30
OVER 30

A T L A N T I

GULF OF MEXICO

Copyright © 1968 by Edwin Scott Gaustad

167

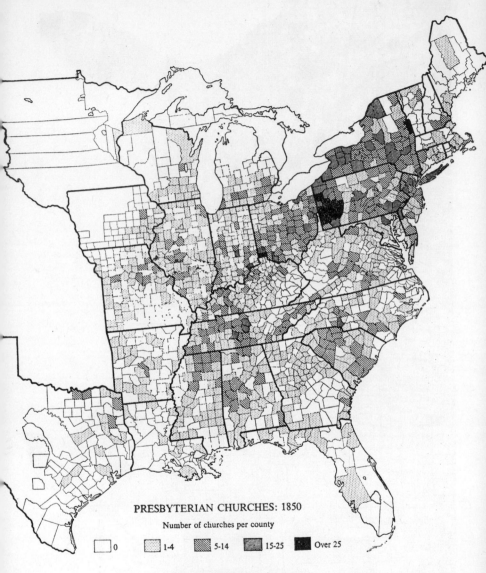

PRESBYTERIAN CHURCHES: 1850

Number of churches per county

0   1-4   5-14   15-25   Over 25

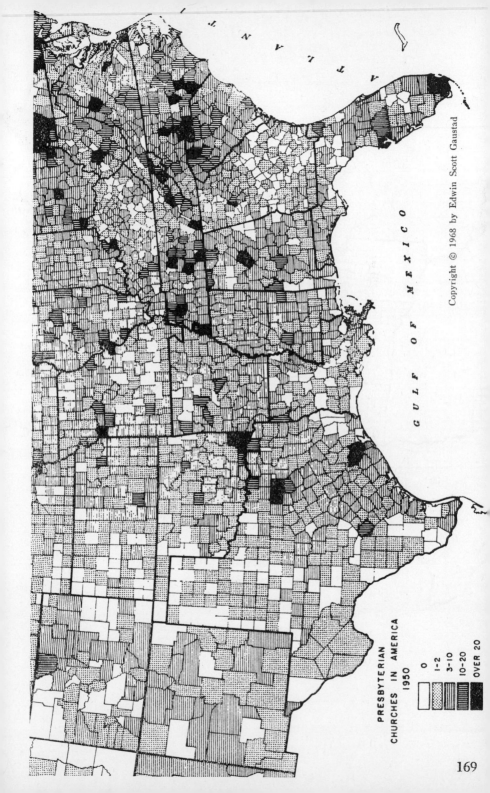

PRESBYTERIAN
CHURCHES IN AMERICA
1950

0
1-2
3-10
10-20
OVER 20

Copyright © 1968 by Edwin Scott Gaustad

169

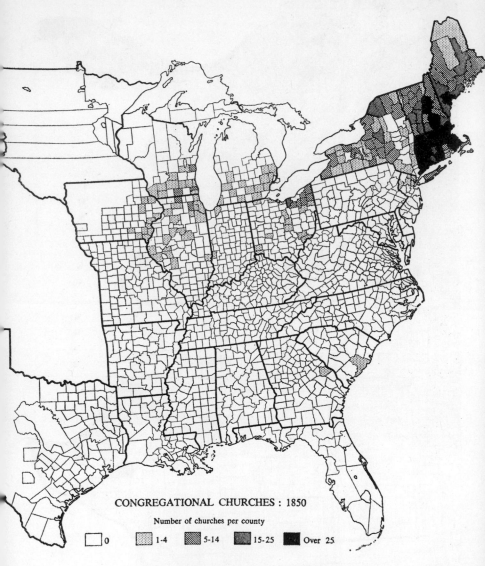

CONGREGATIONAL CHURCHES : 1850

Number of churches per county

☐ 0 ▨ 1-4 ▨ 5-14 ▨ 15-25 ■ Over 25

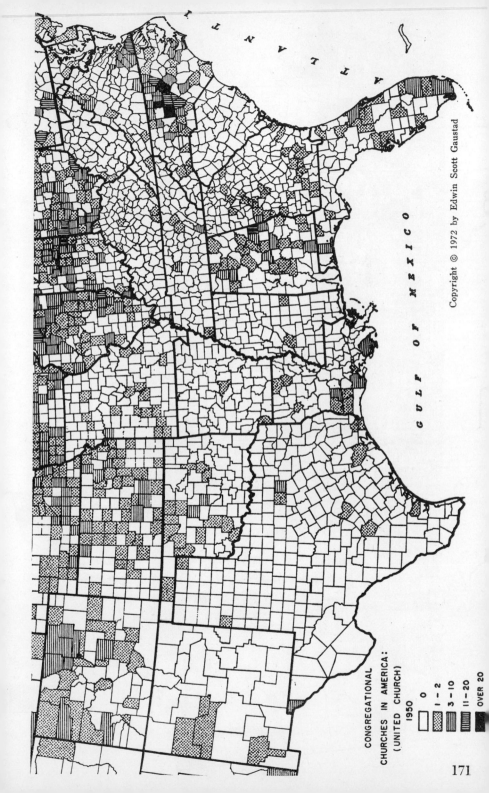

CONGREGATIONAL
CHURCHES IN AMERICA:
(UNITED CHURCH)
1950

0
1 - 2
3 - 10
11 - 20
OVER 20

171

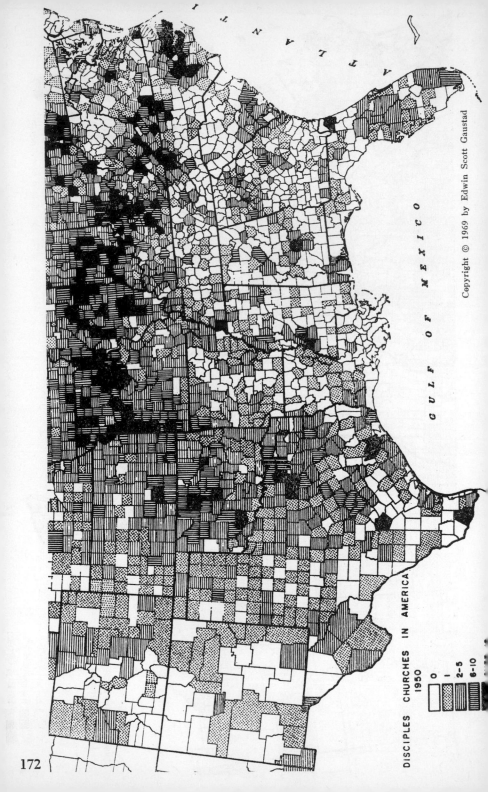

DISCIPLES CHURCHES IN AMERICA
1950

0
1
2-5
6-10

GULF OF MEXICO

Copyright © 1969 by Edwin Scott Gaustad

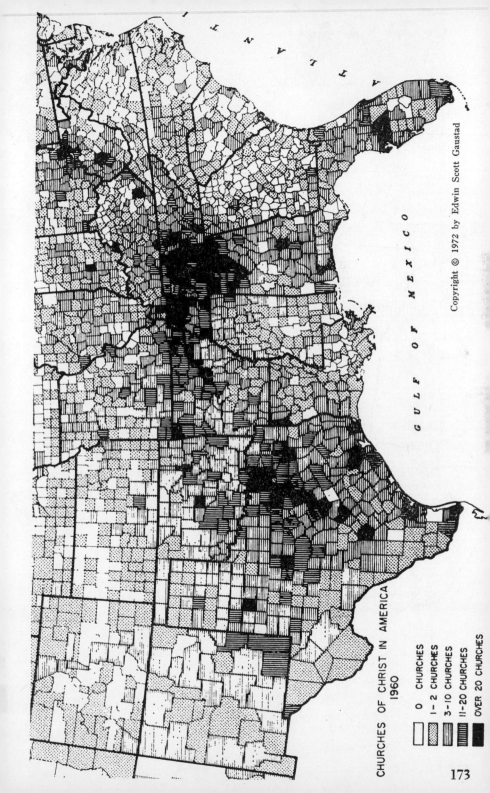

CHURCHES OF CHRIST IN AMERICA
1960

☐   0   CHURCHES

  1- 2   CHURCHES

  3-10   CHURCHES

  11-20   CHURCHES

■   OVER 20   CHURCHES

GULF OF MEXICO

ATLANTIC

Copyright © 1972 by Edwin Scott Gaustad

173

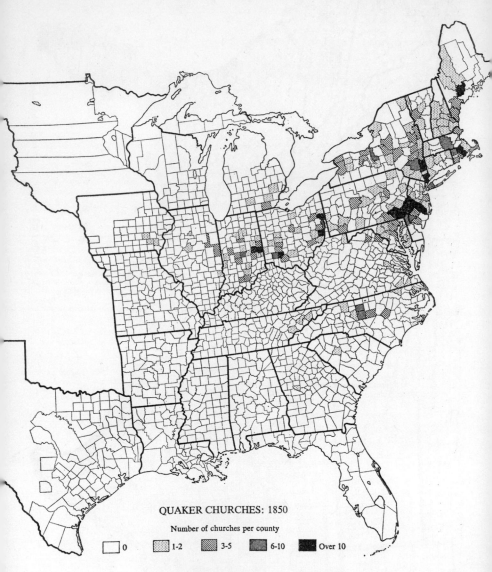

QUAKER CHURCHES: 1850

Number of churches per county

☐ 0   ▨ 1-2   ▨ 3-5   ▨ 6-10   ■ Over 10

Copyright © 1962 by Edwin Scott Gaustad

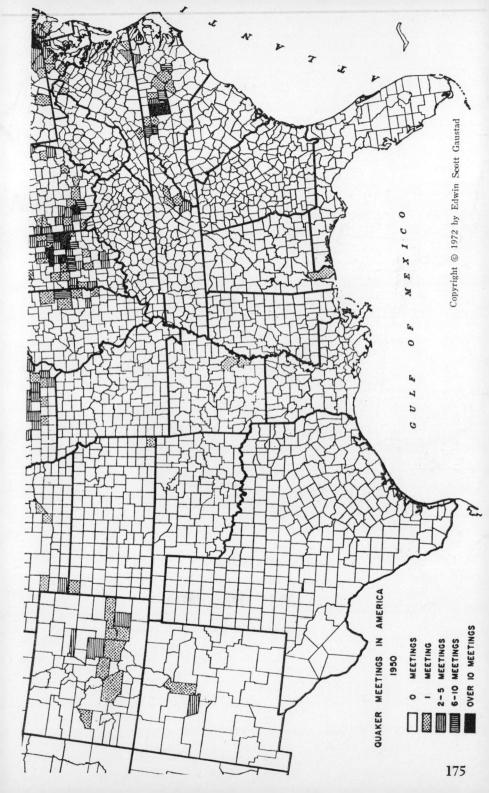

QUAKER MEETINGS IN AMERICA
1950

0   MEETINGS

1   MEETING

2 – 5   MEETINGS

6 – 10   MEETINGS

OVER 10 MEETINGS

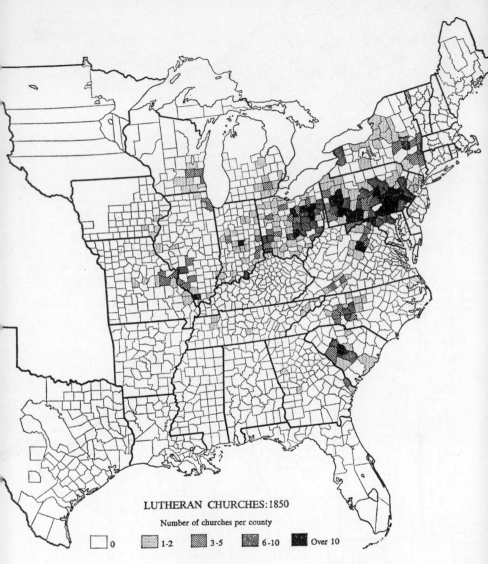

LUTHERAN CHURCHES: 1850

Number of churches per county

0   1-2   3-5   6-10   Over 10

Copyright © 1962 by Edwin Scott Gaustad

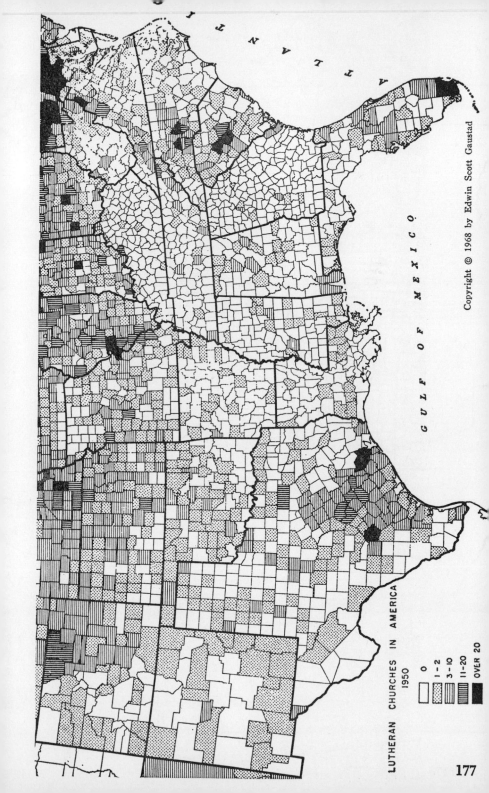

LUTHERAN CHURCHES IN AMERICA
1950

0
1 - 2
3 - 10
11 - 20
OVER 20

Copyright © 1968 by Edwin Scott Gaustad

177

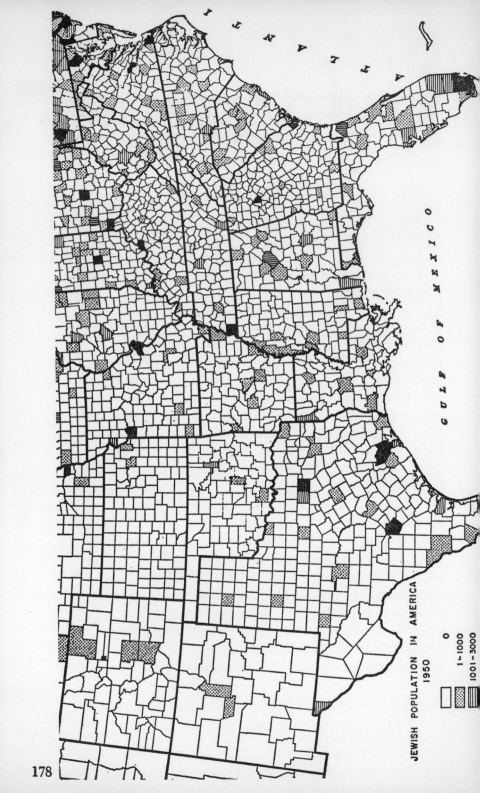

JEWISH POPULATION IN AMERICA
1950

- ☐ 0
- ▨ 1–1000
- ▥ 1001–5000

7
TOWARD A CHARTER FOR A SOUTHERN THEOLOGY

It is a mark of something that this collection of analytic essays includes one effort to sketch out a theological charter for the southern church's belief-practice. The aim here is to outline some contours of a confessional or creedal position which, I hope, honors both the Christian vision of reality by which the churches intend to live and the conditions of the culture in which they exist. As it happens, I share the Christian tradition of the churches, a fact which makes this statement confessional (at least potentially) in a quite literal sense. But novel as the idea might appear to some, there is no sufficient reason why a secularly oriented person or group deeply concerned with the quality of the civilization should not challenge a prevailing theology by charging it with obstructing human development, or with being incapable of attaining its own stated goals, while suggesting some alternative interpretations and correlations.

Clearly, the decision to propose a new charter is predicated on the conviction that a theological position may be dysfunctional for the society in which it operates. Religious absolutists can only bristle when such a contention is put forward, for they are bound to presuppose either that "truth" must be served, whatever the historical consequences may appear to be, or that in the nature of the case there can be no disharmony between what God wills and what is best for man, or both of these. But perhaps greater

179

offense is taken when someone avers that the church's theological position is not "gnosis," a closed-circuit revelation known to no others than true believers, or at least rightly perceived and suitably interpreted only by persons of faith. It just may be that one aspect of the new cultural situation of the 1970s is the acceptance of religious responsibility by the uninitiated, the "great unwashed," that is, by some who admit to a secularist understanding of reality, for providing constructive material for the church's belief and practice. Such an undertaking would hardly concern leaders in societies where the church's influence is nominal, but regions like the American South might profit greatly from the church's receiving secular criticism and contribution. As I say, this scheme is likely to be resisted by particularists, but their hearing it may be a precondition of renewed service and any real power to attract persons to the excellency of the Christian way.

The theologically versed reader will be aware that these introductory comments also touch the doctrine of revelation. The means by which God discloses, man perceives, and the church authorizes has always been a matter of central interest in the Christian tradition. Particularists of Protestant persuasion have classically been wary of "general revelation," that is, of data and formulations which do not derive directly from Scripture. In their eyes, knowledge of God and his will emanate from the context of preaching, creedal affirmation, the devotional life, and "seeing the hand of God in events," with all of these perceptions being based upon and measured by biblical norms. There is an interesting ambiguity on this point in the experience of the rank-and-file of southern churchmen, however, in that the "beauties of nature" are instinctively thought to reveal God—a point for which, by the way, biblical support may be adduced. But typically this has not been the official position of church religion, since religious knowledge has been confined to direct encounter with God in and following upon the experience of salvation. This way of viewing things may be called "differentationist," since people who limit revelation to the company of the saved self-consciously and openly differentiate what they know from any form of generally available insight.

So the proposal with which this chapter began, that the churches listen to secular critiques and constructive alternatives presented by people who do not consciously refine their judgments through a biblical filter, can hardly be acceptable in view of the revelationist bias of southern Protestant orthodoxy. But it is precisely a revision of this orthodoxy that the present quest for a new charter calls for. I am urging that the most searching attention be given to whether orthodoxy works (a strange juxtaposition of noun and verb indeed to the minds of biblicists).

Two considerations lie behind the proposal that orthodoxy's significance and effectiveness be evaluated. The first is the accusation that orthodox religion—in this case, the region's pervasive Evangelical Protestantism, a mixture of positive and negative influences in the past, shows the barest promise of serving southern people well under the conditions of a new cultural situation, some features of which are traced in this chapter. The second, of a quite different order, is that a theological and ecclesiological position, rather than being self-justifying on the basis of appeal to authority, must prove itself historically functional. That is to say, what the church promotes as ultimate truth and prescribes as desirable behavior must result in the cultivation of the noble values of human civilization: the freedom of man's spirit; mutual love and respect; a peaceful society; the dignity of all; the establishment of beneficial institutions and traditions; the creative expression of man's faculties in thought, art, music, literature, drama; significant participation in the affairs of other societies and nations; constructive acknowledgment and rehabilitation of the human propensity for such demonic practices as exploitation, cruelty, and wanton self-aggrandizement in forms and agencies of government. To the extent that these and comparable fruits are not encouraged and enabled to develop, the foundations of the church's program must be judged deficient.

Of course, religious institutions and world views can make certain rich contributions without being held accountable to perform to perfection—whatever "perfection" may mean in an organic context. Moreover, it must always be borne in mind that all social institutions generate both good and evil consequences. Even so, religious orthodoxy of the South has generally been aligned with the causes of conservatism, aesthetic vacuity, anti-intellectualism, provincialism, resistance to new cultural currents, regional self-defense, political and economic reaction, and the inculcation of guilt and inflexibility in man's interior life. It has no greater need than to face up squarely to its own complicity in movements of repression, retrogression, and absolutizing the social status quo. And as I shall endeavor to show, this role has been due in significant part to the belief-system of the churches, not merely to the inevitable failures of religious institutions and communicants, or to the wider facts of life in a southern region which has been poor in matters of economics and range of options.

It is interesting that southern Christians should be so wary of looking beyond or outside orthodoxy on the question of revelation. However unsystematically, they, more than many peoples, must perceive that the fundamental assumption of the biblical message is that God is known by what he shows of himself in this world, among men, through events, in the experience of ordinary people, in moments of gaiety, sadness, and challenge. But even if that fact concerning the biblical view of history has not registered formally in their study of Scripture, they ought to make and probably have made the connection. For Southerners have done a lot of living; they have tasted deeply of family love and warm interpersonal relations in the community; they have taken seriously birth, illness, separation and reunion, death; they have come face to face with economic hardship. Neither concepts nor traditions nor abstractions have governed the southern imagination, but events, transactions, relationships, feelings, and gratifications.*

If this is true of Southerners in the arena of personal, family, and preurban community experience, it is no less characteristic of the corporate regional experience. Years ago C. Vann Woodward in describing the uniqueness of southern history, pointed to the singular experience of this one American region with respect to suffering, defeat, poverty, and isolation from the movements of modern social change.[1] On both personal and societal fronts, it appears, Southerners are prototypical existentialists. Surely living this way provokes acknowledgment of the transparency of earthy events to the depths, to ultimate meaning.

Southerners' continual rendezvous with crisis and their existential way of confronting it, predictably, have rendered the crisis-ethos of Evangelical Protestantism an attractive option and made the average southern churchman more a pietist (of the salvationist sort) than a fundamentalist. But these developments have not concomitantly produced

---

* I am reminded here of Professor Hudson's observations in chapter 5 that the southern fundamentalist belief-system could have been orally transmitted, since the examples his interviewees used in talking about their practice of life are drawn not from the Bible but from everyday life. My observations about the earthiness of southern people concur with his, obviously. But I am contending in this chapter that their penchant for the ordinary and practical makes them very biblical, in the classical sense. A part of their problem is that they have not seen that they live every day in remarkably biblical fashion, in their natural modes of perception and interpretation. Now it is time for them to do away with the rationalist and impositionist views of the Bible which have been standard fare in the popular churches for many decades, thereby squaring their "doing a lot of living" with their religious positions.

an openness to criticism of orthodoxy, as might have been expected. On the theological point of revelation, our present consideration, southern Christians personally have responded to their various inner intimations concerning proclaimed truth. This is why they have been receptive to sermons and creeds that "feel right," for example, those that highlight guilt and pardon, the promise of ultimate deliverance in heaven, and the purity of regional religion. But they have not matched this practice of a "natural" (as distinct from "revealed") knowledge of divine working with a public articulation that the intimation faculty is an appropriate and credible vehicle of perception. Instead they have continued to say, we believe only what is spoken to man in Scripture. I think that in functioning thus, they have failed, in the epistemological area, to capitalize on the richness of their experience. As a result, the teaching done by the churches is a diminishment—and partial falsification—of their knowing so much about living.

In other words, the southern religious tradition has fruitful resources to tap, which it has failed to cultivate to its own benefit. Abundantly available are such primordial qualities as: suffering, pangs of guilt, occasion for humility, a deep-going moral consciousness, a sense of tragedy, the idiom of ultimacy, a sense of human community, and concrete alienation (from Negroes). Such a span of exposure to life, if ever it affected the reigning view of the nature of revelation, could soften and make more compelling and relevant the religious message of the church in the South. That is to say, southern people possess the personal history to enable them to encounter transcendence *within* ordinary experience, as the persons they are. This capacity is remote indeed from orthodoxy where claims and prescriptions are prior to experience and imposed upon it, and may relate to it without dynamic reciprocity. Orthodoxy's formula runs something like: acknowledge revealed truth, and in the process discover life. The alternative view of revelation being proposed here, which I am contending is so friendly to the natural contours of southern existence, is: assault life, and discover ultimate meaning through that vigorous participation. This means allowing the character of life to shape the manner in which revelation, truth, dogma, and authority are conceptualized, with the effect that those objective entities *take the form of* existential experience, as distinct from their being superimposed upon experience. (It seems to me that only some such view of objectivity accords with the fundamental character of Christianity as a truly historical religion, as well as with the actual practice of the church over the centuries. So understood, ordinary experience is rendered holy as both means and depository—indeed the false distinction between how one knows and what is known is transmuted into dynamic process.)

Much of the South's—and traditional Christendom's—problem in this respect has arisen from misconceptions of "truth" and "authority." The standard notion has been for centuries informed by Greek rationality, rather than by the more dynamic biblical vision. In this connection, a contemporary biblical scholar points out the difference between the Hebrew word for truth, *amat*, and its Greek counterpart, *aletheia*. For the Hebrews, truth means dependability, trustworthiness in view of the future. The opposite of *amat* is not falsehood but *sehaqar*, that is, undependability. This means that the Hebrew view of truth points toward the future—one trusts in what God will bring to pass. Truth is conformity with what *will be*, not with what *is*. Accordingly "belief" in biblical thinking has more to do with hope than with credulity.

The Greek concept of truth, *aletheia*, literally means "unhiding." Truth has to do not with the future but with what is, with a timeless realm in which a particular condition is now revealed, and with making a right distinction between being and not-being. The highest truth is an eternally changeless idea.

Later, as the Christian faith moved from its Palestinian beginnings into the Greco-Roman world of the Mediterranean basin, truth began to mean the quality of a proposition that comported with the present structure of being. This transmutation of the Hebrew notion of truth transformed Christian faith into a kind of theistic metaphysic.[2]

The time has come for recovering the Hebrew (biblical) definition of truth. The matter of religious authority must be revised accordingly, along lines which are compatible with this corrected notion of the meaning of truth. Terms like "the authority of the Bible," "the timeless truths of the Bible," and the scholastic version of "the faith once for all delivered to the saints" clearly are inconsistent in tone with truth understood as "trust in what God will bring to pass," dependability, trustworthiness in view of the future. Under the old definition, authority meant the tenacious hold which certain rational concepts rightly possessed for true believers. As a parallel growth, those institutions and officeholders designated as defenders or promoters of the truth were granted watertight power to safeguard orthodoxy. On a quite different tack, suitable convictions were handed down, regulated, and reviewed by higher judicatories like creedal traditions, ordination councils, and church governing bodies. Faithful belief thus became, both officially and typically, a matter for rational pronouncement, superimposition, and subscription. Under these conditions it did not characteristically emerge from living congregations where mutual ministry might have occasioned dynamic revelation, including the formulation of doctrine.

Religious authority, while by no means intelligently regarded as *de novo*, or as confined to the experience of a single individual, congregation, or denomination, should nevertheless be rooted in the living experience of those who acknowledge it. (In certain senses it always is, of course.) That is to say, it should reflect a sense of the community (universal as well as local) and be an empirical dynamic, rather than being a creed or code in the context of a theistic metaphysic. This means it is more akin to an instrumental value than to an asserted end-state. Authority belongs to a quest for arriving at the goal, and is a way of getting there, as distinct from standing as a blueprint of what is alleged to be the exact nature of things. Authority is then associated with compellingness, allurement, and vision, therefore also with risk and unpredictability. Accordingly it shares more with the spirit of creative chaos than of orderly fixity.

With reference to southern churches, such a view of authority, in tandem with truth as dependability, would free Christians to exchange the rigidity and ahistoricality of orthodoxy for a dialectical interaction between Christian tradition and their peculiar experience. Thereby leaders could relax their watchdoggery, while dutiful laymen and skeptical young people could believe more adventurously through the vital inclusion of their daily experiences in the whole span of the faith-life, doctrinal and cultic, as well as practical.

In sum, the entire aim of this proposal is to transform the southern Christian interpretation of revelation, its perception of the ultimate and holy, from something primarily rational and imposed to an existential and historical reality. For this proposal to take root, a holy secularity must inform the unconscious involvement of the people in daily affairs. As such, every major "city" of man's life is to be regarded as an arena in which God delivers his presence, will, and redemption. The same is true of Christian nurture; growth can and does take place across the range of these involvements. Likewise, mission is offered in and through them all, since responsive, loving service is appropriate in them all. One way of listing these several contexts for human living is: family, culture, the political, the economic, the vocational, the religious, the psychophysical, and the imagination.

Elaboration is scarcely required to clarify these various networks of life. In the *family:* we are born; we learn values; sense or do not sense love; acquire a style; find ourselves with a set of obligations; etc. In the *culture:* we are socialized into the values of a people; acquire something of that people's style; form uncriticized assumptions; etc. In the *political:* we learn much about our worth from theory; are delivered duties; play a part in shaping the society's destiny; provide for and learn from public institutions; etc. In the *economic:* we realize basic human needs; plan in order to meet those needs; establish priorities; compete with others; etc. In the *vocational:* we expend most of our working hours; share the sustained company of others; express ourselves; develop basic habits; etc. In the *religious:* we learn our identity and the worth of others; discover our creatureliness; are instructed in noble morality; form basic cosmic images; etc. In the *psychophysical:* we experience pain, sorrow, joy, strength, limitation, power; feel tired, ill-disposed, healthy, vigorous; are rendered capable or incapable in responding to people and situations; etc. In the *imagination:* we structure our perceptions of self, others, nature, relationships, goals, harmony, beauty, worth, etc.

To repeat: revelation, nurture, and mission are engendered in our lives through these several citizenships—whether we participate self-consciously and vigorously or not. It does not help much to say that we learn from and offer service by means of these several citizenships *as they are strained through the biblical message.* Rather, all are themselves sacred vehicles through which reality is apprehended, and through which discipleship is expressed. Mention of the last point magnifies a major merit of this whole view of revelation-truth-authority, for an interpretation of this kind brings organically together "faith" and "works," "revelation" and "service." Instead of being separable, with one prior in schedule and ontological quality, the two are linked, so that, in the very nature of the case, there cannot be revelation without discipleship or worthy service without divine empowerment.

Before treating discipleship directly, however, we must turn from *revelation* to a second theological theme of the proposed new charter, *anthropology*, the doctrine of man. Throughout the preceding discussion, man has been described in historical and dynamic terms as one who lives, changes, reacts, responds, recoils, shapes, is shaped, has relationships, and so on. Specifically, he is the one to whom revelation comes, who has the capacity to perceive meaning in events and relationships, and whose identity equips him as repository of experienced Transcendence.

I suppose that southern orthodoxy would find little fault with any such depiction. However its characteristic images of man belong more to the realm of the essential than the dynamic and to the abstract more than the historical. For the churches present not a picture of man in the ebb and flow of history, but a bipolar still life of reality, the two poles being God and the individual soul. Let us look at these two poles, the *Urstucke*, the primordial components of all reality.

God is construed as "really there," possessing concrete existence, identifiable as if he were body. His authority and his disclosures of truth and man's duty are of a similar order; they smack of realness and concretion, having about them qualities of exactitude and finality. In addition, God is perceived as characteristically and predominantly moral. He is known to be a requiring and demanding being, one who cares about nothing so much as man's behavior. Understanding of *man's* nature and identity must and does correspond to what God is and what he expects of man. As the Father is, so are his children. Man's characteristic moral nature is specifically associated with his being a deficient or defective creature. He is made for rectitude and in rectitude he finds satisfaction, purpose, and everlasting life. God has laid out his way, and man can apprehend it through prayer and spiritual sensitivity.

In the popular southern version of this way of thinking about Christianity, the bipolar image of reality places the morally requiring God over against the morally defective individual soul, with a crucial alienation separating them. A state of "gone-wrongness" prevails. And "state" it is, because it is a morally deficient *status* which identifies the presaved person; that is, he is hopelessly lost. I say "gone-wrongness" because he is askew, misdirected, and doomed to eternal condemnation—unless and until the moment of status-change occurs. Since "Adam's Fall," he has been incapacitated, bereft of moral power to do good and please God. There is "nothing going" between God and himself, either from his natural inclinations or from his responses to the wide world of ordinary experience.

Thus man is fundamentally identified by his not having *status* and his being impotent to achieve *rectitude*. He is a being out of touch, separated, alienated, deficient. At the level of keenest self-awareness, he is the guilty one. By virtue of inherited and deliberate transgression, he is cut off from the state of the good life, here and hereafter. Little wonder then that Christianity spells *rewards and punishments*. There is simply no doubt that the main practical impact of the churches' teaching, whatever the theological intention, is otherworldly status. The religious life is dominated by the desire to avoid hell and gain heaven.

Ingredient in this network of assumptions is a nearly inevitable interpretation of Christ's place in the divine scheme as bridge-builder or agent of atonement. His role is to address the problem: man's guilt, the alienation of man from God, the moral "gone-wrongness" which renders

190

God unaccepting of man and man incommunicado with God. Christ overcomes the separation, and thereby facilitates justification. He is a functionary, one who accomplishes something. By dying, he brings about a status which would be impossible without his crucial (literally, from "cross") intervention.

The most interesting, and ironic, aspect of this theology is that for all its intended and claimed "Christ-centeredness," it has the actual effect of placing man in the position of concerning himself with his own status. The interests of God so dictate and the work of Christ so implements. But there is a second and deeper irony, namely, that the emphasis on the Gospel's being for man, with his welfare in mind, turns out on close examination to be misdirectedly humanistic. Although described as gloriously for man's benefit and perfection, the Christian message is presented in such a way as to prevent a full realization of human development.

So serious a charge demands explication. Although negative results are not intended and certainly do not always result, the southern church's message if taken at face value produces persons with overwrought consciences and excessive moral circumspection. It makes one preoccupied with the degree of his imperfection and superconscious of his decisions. In a word, Christianity so presented identifies man primarily as a person having guilt. If it be objected that guilt is a basic dimension of Christianity whatever its specific interpretation, one has first to concur in that judgment, then proceed to contend that guilt ought to be a casual and constructive quality, not one which lies near the surface to dominate and restrain. Guilt as a feature of the Christian life should serve as an occasion for humility and dependency, rather than as cause for fear, or incentive to constant self-assessment. Guilt ought not point to consignment, or to negative verdict on one's destiny, but to acts which inform one's responsibilities and relationships. The essence of guilt is diminishment— of one's own moral capacity and of others' fulfillment.

Moreover the correlation between guilt-domination and obsession with rewards-punishments is clear. The complex of obligations, feelings, and motives growing out of such a rendering of Christian meaning is likely to build lives which are governed by a sense of duty and a tendency to assess status. Therefore, what is meant to be a redemptive view of the Christian man more often turns out to be restraining, to produce self-consciousness, and to make one a status seeker. Alleged and intended "Christ-centeredness" easily shades off into fearful self-centeredness. In the experience of those who give only partial commitment, yet live nevertheless with the obligation to mind their status, the religious life becomes a matter of consciously doing enough to achieve that status, but is lacking in any deep-going sense of liberation or enjoyment. Under those conditions, the religious life is captured by such expressions as "I hope I'm saved" or "we're all working for the same place" or "religion is like fire insurance in that you'd better get it before you need it."

Despite its essentially anxiety-producing and compartmentalizing tendencies, the southern church's emphasis on guilt has the potential for cultivating serious spirituality. This theme does acknowledge that man's life is meant to be and may be on a higher plane. It encourages uplift and nobility by pointing man beyond himself, the ephemeral, and the material to something transcendent and ultimately moral. Thus goodness is known as a quality which is not automatic or easily come by. Nor is it identical with ordinary human consensus about what is genuinely valuable. Such a conception of goodness stands in judgment upon any particular temporal opinions about what is excellent by referring all such matters to ultimate norms. The prevalence of guilt in church teaching is an appropriate response to the religious life, and stands as a resource laden with constructive potential in southern life.

The third theme, following revelation and anthropology, is *discipleship*, also very close to the heart of regional religious convictions. This is due to the utter seriousness southern churchmen attach to the two major aspects of Christian discipleship: the calling to be a disciple—a learner, one who bears the yoke, the faithful follower—and the evangelistic mission to "make disciples" of the entire human population. In the southern context those two hallmarks of the Christian life have been construed in rather distinctive ways.

The first, the calling to be a disciple is defined in terms of status, behavior (principally moralistic), and compliance with the evangelistic mandate. At the most basic level, the churchman *is* a disciple, that is, he possesses certain knowledge that he has passed from one state of existence, lostness and condemnation *vis-à-vis* God, to a new state, where guilt is pardoned and heaven is guaranteed. On this side of its connotation, then, the "learner" or "yoke-bearer" idea, which is the textual meaning of disciple, is not embodied in southern Protestant practice. One who is or has may hardly be characterized as a learner. On the contrary, discipleship as status suggests arrival, the absence of risk, and a rather precise identity. Discipleship on this showing is more nearly a possession than a learning. However, in another respect southern Christians do exemplify classical discipleship in that they submit to harnessing by seeking to grow in the life of practical obedience. It is correct to say that behavior is one form being a disciple takes in southern imagery. One "disciplines" himself by intense appraisal of the values and practices of his life, purging those patterns which debilitate and nurturing those which by pleasing God build up the soul.

Moreover in connection with their yearning to comply with the evangelistic mandate, southern churchmen seek to show how serious is their commitment to discipleship. They are told that "witnessing" is the highest goal and achievement of the Christian life. Those most pliable to church teaching want earnestly to tell others how to become Christians, thereby to serve as the agency and encouragement for others' experiencing conversion and regeneration. To be sure, a small minority actually express their discipleship in this overt manner. But the task of winning souls is held up as the epitome of Christian activity, since in God's eyes all men *must* be saved. The calling to be an effective instrument is regarded as the noblest grace. The counsels of perfection here are not poverty, chastity, and obedience, but soul-winning first and moralistic behavior second.

But what of the majority which is not "disciplined" to "bring in the sheaves"? We may conjecture that they abstain for a wide variety of reasons, ranging from timidity, to fear, to indifference, to the view that this is the minister's responsibility, to inarticulateness. I suspect that for many there is a dim suspicion that this is neither the most suitable means for making true disciples, nor the appropriate preoccupation of Christian living. Perhaps—it is difficult to say so with finality—those earnest southern churchmen who cannot bring themselves to *verbal* witnessing are restrained by an unformulated awareness that life's problems and disorientations are deeper-going than a relatively simple cure can provide. It is appropriate to return to the refrain, Southerners have done a lot of living; they have seen life in the raw, directly and indirectly. It would be consistent with their experience to doubt that assent to right doctrine (concerning sin, atonement, and salvation) accompanied by a dramatic moment of truth and release can set things right, even on principle. Besides, Southerners have daily opportunity to face such fundamental perversity as poverty, discrimination, and ignorance, so that many may be dissuaded from concentrating all their moral energies on saving souls, despite what they hear from the pulpits or read in denominational literature. Empirically before theologically, they have sensed that evangelism (in this more restricted usage) is one ministry among other ministries. Christians have many opportunities and obligations toward their fellows, and making disciples is only one of them. Moreover, many seem to sense that the evangelistic ministry must possess a total quality; after all, verbality is inadequate because it is only one human mode. Numbers perceive that a caring relationship is absolutely necessary as context for any presentation of the Gospel, and that any form of contact which is capable of consummation and cessation is far too superficial to issue in a new direction.

The task of evangelism is conceived of by the southern church in short-run terms. The disciple is to bear his verbal witness, kindly and gently to be sure, but with a primary view to the "verdict" (literally, the "truth-saying"), until the lost person subscribes. As the process is understood, it terminates. One strongly suspects that Southerners, and people in general, recognize that this rhythm is different from life's. A far more credible and compelling rhythm of Christian ministry was recently described by one working with disadvantaged children in an American city: "We have turned from a crusade—'Free the children immediately, Lord, immediately'—into a mission that might involve us for the rest of our days." Another, engaged in the same service, declared that the group learned "as did Moses and Aaron, that if we really want to set the children free, we will have to stay at it, and at it, and at it. Pharaoh has to be shown." [3] This kind of commitment to a never-ending ministry, so authentically characteristic of human need and the cadence of historical change, is largely foreign to the rhythms of southern evangelism.

The central issue in southern discipleship today is how to correlate "evangelism" and social ministries. Changing conditions within and pressures from the general society have forced the churches to reassess their responsibilities. Contemporary leadership is coming to realize that evangelism is not enough, that it does not exhaust, or maybe even fulfill, Christian vocation. Denominations, congregations, and individuals are called to become involved in meeting the very real needs of people, in the South and everywhere, most of which are not religious in the narrow sense of that word. Yet there is a haunting fear that hearty participation in social ministries would divert the main energies of the Christian cause. Unable, nevertheless, to shield their eyes from secular need and to resist pressure to address human pain, they formulate their mission in terms of both-and: we must retain the primacy of evangelism; at the same time we must minister to all people in the variety of their needs. It is worth noting, however, that neither local church nor denominational budgets reflect much devotion to the latter.

Any sensitive charter for southern theology in the 1970s must deliver at this fundamental point, namely, the correlation of evangelistic and social ministries. First, it must do this by dismissing that way of posing the issues. In this endeavor toward developing a charter we have already touched on that point by mention of the axiom that evangelism must be seen as one ministry among other ministries. There is the obvious implication here that the Christian God is primarily concerned that people achieve fulfillment by living abundant and responsible lives rather than that people meet an obligation or find a center in line with any particular Christian formulation of the experience of ultimacy. Recognition of that is a crucial place to begin.

Beyond that, it must be seen that rigid distinctions between personal and social dimensions of experience and between sacred and secular realities cannot really be maintained. One surely is not a Christian, first personally, then socially, since whatever his experience, it is mediated to him by relationships and cultural symbols. To be sure, one is a center of valuing decisions and acts, but his identity is not describable as something which has happened to him in isolation. In other words, Christian identity can best be viewed as process, or growth, or movement toward a goal, rather than as status, which surely is an ahistorical way of identifying anyone. This is to say that an adequate theology does not require that a person be something before he can do something. Instead, one *is becoming*—becoming is what one is, and a primary mode of becoming is doing. To paraphrase an old theological slogan, we might say that engagement with life is a converting ordinance. Notice, *engagement* with *life*, not participation in churchly things, merely or as such, constitutes the pilgrimage. Therefore secular and sacred collapse into a single realm of experience which is where man lives and where alone his salvation can be hammered out. It follows also from the previous discussion that to schedule stages in the dynamic becoming process is simply inappropriate. The church cannot say, therefore, first be saved, then "discipline" yourself. Rather, it must enliven the full reality of each person, being concerned to minister to all his own needs and make him responsive to all those of other persons as well. In a real sense, to be saved is to be oblivious to the question, am I saved, in favor of concentration on growth, one's own and others', toward abundant and responsible living.

To summarize, the church misses the mark when it debates between evangelism and social ministries, or makes the two separate and obligatory, when it demarcates the sacred from the secular, when it judges status to be the precondition of behavior, or when it schedules the sequence by which one attains to salvation. Furthermore, the church takes the easy way out when it interprets its mission as the striving to bring to pass a single event in a person's life. For any view of Christian responsibility which can program a cessation of ministry to a person (in this case, because the goal was reached when he was saved), or limit its outreach to the Christianization of an outsider, is by that measure deficient—and irresponsible. When those models operate, the agency appears as salesman, not minister.

The movement to a fourth area, *conversion*, follows smoothly upon discipleship; in fact, one of the hallmarks of discipleship as interpreted by southern religious leadership is the proximity of the two. This point has never been made more cogently than by Professor Langdon Gilkey:

Some groups, notably in our day the Southern Baptists, have made evangelism the central core of the church, and their experience reveals the problem involved. For then ministers tend to be taught, not how to care for their flock by preaching, counseling, and worship, but how to evangelize—i.e., how to persuade other people to join the flock. And when these new members ask, "Now that I have joined, what am I to do?" the answer is apt to be "Go out among your neighbors and bring in some more"—who, presumably, will in turn themselves merely seek new additions among their neighbors. Being a Christian thus becomes merely the operation of expanding itself. And with this the religious reality of Christianity, both as a personal relation to God through the hearing of His Word and the worship of His glory, and the incarnating of that Word in acts of love and reconciliation, is in danger of being lost.[4]

In many quarters of the southern Protestant church, it is the moment, or at least the alleged fact, of entry into the Christian life which is emphasized. The sequential image which we have already considered operates here too; "one must be born before he can grow" is the kind of logic frequently employed. In succumbing to the "new birth" metaphor, the southern church does not act peculiarly since failure to perceive that metaphor is a common human failing. But this particular reification is dramatically important since it allows the church to place entry or initiation—the act of conversion—in a class by itself. As before, dynamic or organic depictions of the religious life are thereby ruled out. Consequently, despite much well-intentioned talk about growth, the real commitment of the church is to winning souls, even through its teaching agencies.

In this connection, it is intriguing that hundreds of thousands of Southerners continue to attend church services religiously when almost every sermon they hear treats a topic which is by definition irrelevant to their situation. That is to say, in Baptist and sectarian churches typically, and among Methodist churches frequently, the majority of sermons is directed toward the salvation of lost souls, especially in Sunday evening services. We must inquire into why the churches manage to attract those for whom conversion has already been accomplished when the appeal of the sermon is to repent and be saved? In coming to terms with this question, we may be probing rather deeply into the southern religious culture.

Here are some possible explanations for the attraction of evangelistic sermons to those already saved. (1) The converted Southerner may be little more than self-serving anyway. That is, he may envisage the Christian life as largely a matter of status. Having attained the desired standing, the promise of heaven after death, he is now primarily concerned to pay an obligation, and going to church is one part of that obligation. What is said in the church service is of small importance to him; he pays a minimum of attention to the entire occasion. (2) Particularly in the case of revival meetings, something of a dramatic air prevails, with the result that some attend to see who will cross the line, passing "from death unto life." When people are converted, there may be a sense of festivity, accompanied perhaps by catharsis, on the part of worshipers who are primarily onlookers. (3) In simple cultures especially, ritual reenactment is a staple of life. A mode of public gathering may need merely to be familiar. One returns over and over because he wants to participate in something he knows and associates with a basic sense of well-being.

But there are more serious explanations for the evangelistic habituation of many southern churchmen. (4) One suspects that not many genuinely sensitive Christians can really believe that the life of redemptive relationship to God and neighbor is punctual rather than linear. Surely anything so relational and ultimate, they may reason, dimly probably, must carry with it risk, growth, the possibility of cooling, and the need for renewal. Consequently they have need for continually being reconfirmed and reassured. Knowing that human relationships are of an on-again, off-again character, they intuit that man's relation to God, being comparably dynamic, is similar. Thus a person keeps on listening to sermons which are intended to impress upon others their estrangement from God in order to find credibility in the official conviction that he himself is among the saved.

(5) When this point is extended into the social realm, the sating of Southerners' great need for legitimation, a point stressed in chapter 2, comes to the surface. While listening to sermons differentiating the spiritual haves from the have-nots, they see the human race in terms profoundly endemic to the southern consciousness, the distinction between the in-group and the out-group. The evangelistic modality—a vital part of its theological substance—resonates to southern experience. Churchgoers keep on hearing that humanity is differentiated, a fact which they have learned from their ordinary experience of distinguishing Southernness from all other cultural identifications. By implication, the evangelistic sermons commend the in-group, those who have undergone conversion, saying to them both individually and corporately as Southerners that a comparison of themselves with other persons and societies places them at advantage.

(6) Surely this preoccupation of many of the popular churches with evangelism is a means of avoiding other matters of importance. By putting all their money on the ingathering of souls, the southern churches can justify inattention to the moral stresses of the society, most dramatical-

ly its historic racial situation. At the danger of a very cynical interpretation, one wonders if the unexpressed logic of much southern religious leadership could run: we must save souls so that we won't have to put the South's house in order. This is a far cry from the official position that all of what God wills to happen is packed into the commission to convert the lost, both because God's moral sense is inherently satisfied thereby and because without converted hearts the fruits of the Spirit cannot be cultivated.

If the foregoing analysis of the role of conversion in southern religious life is at all accurate, the retention of conversion as a major doctrine-objective would appear to be of questionable value. To the contrary. While the benefits of conversion have been limited largely to the private self and his station in the world to come, it does not follow inexorably that the theme of conversion is bankrupt. What is needed is not the deletion but the reclamation of this component. Its focus should be shifted from the status concerns of the private self to the person as one in community with other persons, and from life in the world-to-come to embodying creative good will in one's ordinary activities. It is odd that a metaphor like conversion (*metanoia*) which is so implicitly rich in *moral* meaning should have taken on a nearly exclusive ontic significance. Moreover it is ironic, if also explicable, that a southern society so intent on devising "new" programs aimed at secular transformation of the region should have failed to capitalize on this powerful concept of change so central in its religious arsenal. (But again, see chapter 2.)

Conversion must take place, if at all, where one lives, that is, within the historical circumstances of people's living. It cannot refer to an abstraction. Being overwhelmingly moral in connotation, it rightly refers to behavior here and now, not to transactions between heaven and earth or to a changed countenance on the part of the Eternal Judge looking down upon erring man. Briefly, I will suggest five areas of southern living within which true conversion might assert itself. One would be a shift from nonchalant to critical ways of viewing one's own and the society's accustomed patterns. For example, deep stirring of moral sensibilities would be indicated if churchmen began to question the propriety of rigidly segregated neighborhoods, whether the decisive value were race, class, or economics. Perhaps life would be enriched for all if (without dispensing with zoning regulations) children from various classifications lived close enough to play together. A second possible indicator of conversion might be the reorientation of churchmen's lives from private to public concerns, that is, greater involvement of time and moral commitment to public affairs in the local community, as against "minding one's own business." This in turn leads to a third fundamental change, the development of friendship with people other than one's "own kind." We could rightly conclude that some genuine alteration were taking place if a person or family in choosing friends replaced comfort and status as the primary determinants with the yearning to know and enhance other kinds of people. A fourth area is the matter of being converted from a success ethic to a contribution ethic. When there is evidence that an individual in our society where work and rewards are considered inherently good reconceives of his employment as a means of enhancing human life, we are likely to infer that something dramatic has happened. Closely related as a fifth indicator is the movement occasionally seen in a person's life from domination by safety and security to the willingness to risk. Ironically, to say risk is to intimate faith, faith demonstrated in basic life-style and in valuing. This kind of faith-living is surely much closer to the Christian ideal than is faith in doctrine or in one's own salvation.

This brings us to the fifth and final article in the charter being proposed in this chapter, namely, *models of the Christian life*. At the outset it will be useful to develop a lexicon of words and images having frequent and, usually, uncritical currency in southern religious circles. Some of these principal symbols of the culture are: duty, guilt, achievement, striving, sacrifice, self-consciousness, logic, certainty, authority. Diverse as they are, I think we may generalize about them to say that they highlight the churches' concentration on growing a constituency which is, perhaps paradoxically, both self-conscious and bold. The typical product of the churches, if their priorities and rhetoric prevail, would be an individual who is aware of his violations of God's law, concerned to be pardoned, conscious of his duty, zealous for converting others, loyal to the institutional church, accepting of biblical, denominational, and pastoral authority, and forthright in his personal claim to Christian identity.

I want to stress the degree of self-consciousness which this notion of Christian identity carries with it. One ought to be vigorously confident that he is saved, eager to enable others to live with this same assurance, and anxious to brand his status, his actions, and the institutions he supports as Christian. In other words, this style of Christian identity is calculated and demonstrative. Alternative ways of conceiving of the Christian style, not prominent in the South, cluster about casual. There "casual" is a pejorative description of the religious life. The notion that one could be casual and serious is as alien a way of thinking as that one can read the Bible seriously without reading it literally. "Serious," then, means with intensity, consciously, taking care to indicate who is doing the deed or speaking the word and to what end the action is directed. The tasks to be done are clear, they are to be undertaken boldly, and accomplishment is to be expected; there is little of subtlety, patience, or hope.

When the religious disposition is programmed in this manner, we would hardly anticipate that the kinds of achievements resulting from a process of aging would flourish; for example, views of evangelism, religious education, and the general nurture of Christian lives which presuppose that these are lifetime processes of growth. Let us recall the "preach for the verdict" mandate commonly articulated in the southern church. This same habit of mind carries over into much Sunday school teaching, many educational programs, and even in informal pastoral counseling. The assumption is that whatever needs to be done can and must be done by prompt and forthright decision-action. Accordingly, church architecture, to cite one instance, has been regarded as having secondary importance. This depreciation is also due to the fact that the patience threshold of southern minds is ill-suited to the longsuffering care which achievements in aesthetic areas require.

Similarly, the fashioning of models of Christian *morality* has not been a distinguished contribution from the southern religious context. Perhaps this is surprising in view of the inordinate hold morality has on these minds. But creative, innovative, and contextually sensitive forms of the moral life have been missing. Some possible instances are: constructive race relations built on the contacts between blacks and whites; fresh thinking about the positive values inherent in an essentially agrarian society; capitalizing on the tenacity of religious authority over Southerners' minds to engage in reformulations of traditional Christianity (which is, modestly, the ambition of this essay). But the cultivation of rich moral forms is a fine art, taking vast quantities of patience and perceptiveness.

In the contemparary era, new sensibilities are appearing and being accredited by major sectors of the society. These range from new modes of music among the young, to more purposive interpretations of human sexuality, to growing recognition of the importance of feelings in organizational behavior, and so on. Remarkably, all these changes have affinity with the historic southern sensibilities. In the case of the first, country music and gospel songs have both been composed and widely accepted by the people of the South.

Tonally, not a great deal would be necessary for this musical sensibility to be transposed into the key of folk or rock music. With respect to the emergence of new sensibilities in general, Southerners have a running start on a number of fronts because of their personalist, rather than rationalist, approach to life. One wishes their theology and church programs were as vital and dynamic as many of the human qualities which characterize their ordinary flights of imagination and their daily social interactions.

Often any reference to religious symbols produces a tightening effect on Southerners, both the dedicated and the heavenly status seekers. That is, for all the vitality and soft piety of their experience, they see religion in terms of their own guilt and the divine demands to which they must be dutifully responsive. Whereas their moods and sensibilities should, ideally, give rise to the colorful and the dangerous, in fact the religious life is more likely to be somewhat sterile and antiseptic. Often missing from the religious life, sometimes misdirectedly present, are beauty, joy, freedom, risk, celebration, and the casual spirit. I am appealing for the establishment of some (at least) continuity between the loveliness of much of their ordinary living and their formal religious life.

As a final approach to models of the Christian life, we may ask, how does the South envisage sainthood? Surely the category of saint affords us with one of the more helpful signals for discerning the values resident within any religious culture.

In the imagination of southern Christians, a saint is typically female, past middle age, white, southern in manner, and gregarious. Such a person is not usually conspicuous by qualities of glamor, sophistication, or public-mindedness. With reference to glamor, "she" is not apt to be memorable in appearance or erotically attractive. One suspects that were "she" evocative of male sexuality her image would be tarnished. In other words, "she" is not likely to be perceived in corporeal terms. "She" must be a challenge to no one, especially those who confer sainthood upon her. "She" cannot rival or parallel the aspirations to glamor, of whatever sort, felt by more earthly people.

On the subject of sophistication, little is expected of the southern saint. Her standing is not acquired by the display of cultivated insight. During discussions of issues, whether in parlor or church conference, her role is likely to be that of silent (but strong) presence, or personal, as distinct from ideological, peacemaker. Her direct contributions are to individuals, not institutions, to personal feelings and needs, not to the substantive grasp of issues which divide people and determine policy. Closely related is the third quality, public-mindedness. Since her life is lived ideally in the domain of personal relationships, her expected role performance does not include involvement in the political activities of the community, or in advocacy of social change. In fact "she" would betray her role were "she" to promote a cause vigorously or display partisanship in public affairs. Her life is spent supporting individuals and groups through personal acts of kindness and charity. Identification with others, rather than political efforts in their behalf, heads the list of her admirable attributes.

I think we can characterize the southern model of saintliness along four lines. The first two have already been intimated, namely, personality type, and altruism in the form of personal service. "She" is gentle, kindly, soft-spoken, supportive—the kind of person in whose presence you "feel good." Her concern for others is expressed by the sacrificial giving of time and money in behalf of the needs of individuals and groups in her community. "She" is not known as a champion of the rights of others, or as community organizer, or as political activist. (It may even be that her chosen means for changing the world is through the conversion of individuals, typically by "soft-sell" and "low-key" methods, but this is usually accompanied by altruistic service.)

Thirdly, "she" is a firm believer in orthodox doctrine. Whereas not given to theological hair-splitting or even open defense of traditional dogma, "she" does not concern herself with fresh, innovative thinking about the Christian message. Her style is to practice it, in her own mode, rather than to engage in probing its depths of meaning, thereby opening the way to new church interpretation and ministry. It cannot be said of this model that a saint is "one who goes to the borderline of belief and unbelief."

The final characteristic of the southern saint is faithfulness to the institutional church. "She" is there whenever the doors open. Few aspects of the church's life mean more to her than small prayer groups, the congregation's weekly service for prayer, the missionary society, and fellowship occasions. "She" is loyal to her pastor, gives generously of her income, keeps herself informed of denominational affairs, and loves all the children of the world. The church is by all odds the primary agency of social participation in her life.

The pluralization of models for sainthood is an eventuality which will herald a new day for the religious culture of the South—and the southern culture at large. When publicly oriented as well as privately oriented churchmen emerge, and their contributions are adjudged as saintly, the church will enlarge its ministry and enhance its power to attract courageous people. The time is coming when southern saints will include male, highly partisan persons (bearded like their spiritual prototypes of biblical times?) who are more inclined to universal than regional norms. They may well be the sorts of persons (of both genders) who will speak out, aggressively seek change, and work to alter structures. Ecclesiastically, they may not teach Sunday school, see their own denomination as the primary reference group, or engage in daily devotionals. I am not suggesting that the older model is fraudulent or passé, however; rather that there are, and will be, alternatives to it which are at least as authentic.

Throughout this essay in empirical theology, a significant current has run barely beneath the surface. It is the observation that the South, because of its very lagging behind in technological and urban development, is now in a position to reclaim and give guidance to the entire nation. How different this is from the past 175 years when the region has been preoccupied with solving its own problems! While disassociating myself from the tradition of New South boosterism, I believe that the church of the South ought to take its place near the center of that position: it has multitudes of people, a monopoly on the governing idiom of existence, unbelievable vitality, and deep reservoirs of concern and good will. Perhaps even that destiny-consciousness which hitherto has been so large a part of its problem, can now be turned to ultimate effectiveness by helping lead a whole society to a more nearly realized kingdom of God on earth.

NOTES

1. C. Vann Woodward, *The Burden of Southern History* (Baton Rouge: Louisiana State University Press, 1960), chap. 1.

2. I am indebted to Harvey G. Cox for this report of the analysis of Professor Klaus Koch on "The Hebrew Truth Concept in Greek Language." See "Non-Theistic Commitment," *Cross Currents*, XIX (Fall, 1969), 403-4.

3. Elizabeth O'Connor, *Journey Inward, Journey Outward* (New York: Harper, 1968), p. 157.

4. Langdon Gilkey, *How the Church Can Minister to the World Without Losing Itself* (New York: Harper, 1963), p. 64n.